THE

CHARLESTON

"FREEDMAN'S COTTAGE"

THE

CHARLESTON
"FREEDMAN'S COTTAGE"

AN ARCHITECTURAL TRADITION

Lissa D'Aquisto Felzer

FOREWORD BY HARLAN GREENE

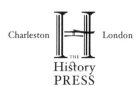

Charleston · London

THE
History
PRESS

Published by The History Press
Charleston, SC 29403
www.historypress.net

Cover design by Natasha Momberger

First published 2008

Manufactured in the United States

ISBN 978.1.59629.286.4

Library of Congress Cataloging-in-Publication Data
Felzer, Lissa.
The Charleston freedman's cottage : an architectural tradition / Lissa Felzer.
p. cm.
Includes bibliographical references and index.
ISBN 978-1-59629-286-4
1. Freedmen--Dwellings--South Carolina--Charleston--History. 2. African Americans--
Dwellings--South Carolina--Charleston--History. 3. Historic buildings--South Carolina--
Charleston. 4. Cottages--South Carolina--Charleston. 5. Architecture, Domestic--South
Carolina--Charleston. 6. Charleston (S.C.)--Buildings, structures, etc. 7. Charleston
(S.C.)--History. 8. Freedmen--South Carolina--Charleston--Biography. 9. African
Americans--South Carolina--Charleston--Biography. 10. Charleston (S.C.)--Biography.
I. Title.
F279.C49N424 2008
728'.373089960730757915--dc22
2008037235

Notice: The information in this book is true and complete to the best of our knowledge. It is offered without guarantee on the part of the author or The History Press. The author and The History Press disclaim all liability in connection with the use of this book.

This book is dedicated to Joseph Paul D'Aquisto Sr.
Wherever you are, we miss you.

CONTENTS

Contents

FOREWORD

Charleston has long been defined (and some would say obsessed) by its boundaries. Early on it was protected by a thick brick wall along the Cooper River, with moats and earthworks along its other three sides. To gain entry or leave, there was a drawbridge controlling access near the present-day corner of Broad and Meeting Streets. When, more than three hundred years after its first construction, parts of the old wall were uncovered under a cobbled street, the news excited much curiosity. Charleston historians and citizens flocked to see the remnants of the old lines that once demarcated the proud old city. Though those walls were taken down by the expanding town, many new ones, metaphorical and real, were raised over the years. At the time of the Revolution, a protective hornwork was built across the current Marion Square and the city eventually saved a bit of the venerable structure and enshrined it behind a protective iron fence for all to see. Defensive lines farther north are remembered today in the location named for them: Line Street. Similarly, for a few generations, a street called Boundary was the northernmost limit of Charleston, which became a corporate entity in 1783. Laws that applied to the south side of the street had no power beyond it. That demarcation line between the city and "the neck," and between law and lawlessness, shifted about 1850, when Boundary's name was changed to Calhoun in honor of statesman John C. Calhoun, who died that year. This was when the city nearly doubled in physical size. City limits were pushed up the neck to the present-day Mount Pleasant Street.

Ten years later, in 1860, the City of Charleston and the American South drew a metaphorical line in the sand. South Carolina dissolved old political boundaries, seceding from the Union in 1860, following Calhoun's political philosophy. The Civil War started on a small man-made island named Fort Sumter in the harbor, though perhaps it would have been more fitting to have had it centered instead on another one of the city's "palm-crowned isles" (in Civil War poet Henry Timrod's phrase): the more aptly named Folly. The war was a bad gamble for Charleston; it spelt ruin. The city went down in defeat and lay in a state of decay for decades. It furled its banners, shut its doors and put up emotional and defensive barriers against the victorious North. The city sulked; it did not expand its limits (and some would say its horizons) for another century.

By the time America came to mark the centennial of the Civil War, other lines and limits had solidified and had come to define and bind Charleston in its own mind and that of popular imagination. Walls as invisible as those buried under the streets had become inviolate; their effects, like those of an unseen force field, were palpable and real. It was said of proud old Charleston that its social barriers were impregnable and could not be breached; within them lived gracious aristocrats in their tall, if narrow, single houses turned sideways to the street, personifying a civilization that was ideal. Everyone was wealthy and well-mannered. If folks had to work it was just because they had all lost their fortunes in "the War" (as if there had only ever been one), known as "the recent unpleasantness." "North side manners" were observed by not peering from windows on the north or east side of your house, to allow privacy to neighbors with gardens and piazzas facing south or west. (Early on, Charlestonians had learned to turn their houses, like sailing ships, into the wind, to catch the prevailing southwesterly breeze blessing summer afternoons and offering a slight respite from the heat.) And just as you did not look out of your windows, there was no reason to gaze beyond the cradling rivers, the Cooper and the Ashley, which defined peninsular Charleston, whose worldview had become insular. Copernicus might have thought differently, but Charleston was the center of the universe. Tourists and gawkers, drawn to town by the charming old stories and equally charming old buildings, were expected to want to peer in—for a small fee.

This was the pact that Charlestonians made with time; don't tell our secrets and we'll keep up the myth of the beauty of history. And for years no doubters appeared. Charlestonians continued to take their bourbon with water, she-crab soup with sherry and iced tea with sugar. They preferred their version of history just as syrupy sweet. Only the graceful and the glorious had ever reigned here. These fanciful stories were told so often that they turned to stone and the old beliefs congealed. Although there was proof everywhere that this was not so, people averted their eyes discreetly; no one seemed to notice the slave quarters (euphemistically called carriage houses or servant quarters) attached to nearly every historic property. It would take years for us to address the issue of the city's long-held African American majority. Similarly, no one expressed an interest in the lower-class whites who lived in those neighborhoods we often had to pass through to get to the world south of Broad Street. Because these were not beautiful, we believed they need not concern us and were not worthy of study.

But ingrained old attitudes like that are changing. And though you can still take tours of Charleston that never mention anything that happened after 1865, nevertheless, as this book attests, there is a new school of thought opening up here.

Driven by curiosity, historians and writers like Lissa Felzer are pushing the old boundaries. They are opening our eyes to so much of the old city that we have never deigned to examine before.

The houses she writes of are not those of the great aristocrats, but of those who worked for them in one way or another and kept their city going. They were not built before the Revolutionary War, though some are antebellum; most were built between 1880 and the early years of the twentieth century. They are not grand, but modest; they seem miniscule versions of the single houses that dot the city. These smaller samples, some just five hundred or so square feet, just like those earlier architectural archetypes, have two realities. There is the physical shell made mostly of wood but some of concrete (the author celebrates a bit of unknown Charleston's architectural history), and there is the soul of the structure—the story of the families that have lived in it and endowed the walls with a patina we call history.

So for the first time, we can cross boundaries into new parts of town to explore, and there are new conclusions about the fabric of Charleston to consider, too. For just as the merchant princes built on East Bay and Meeting, and planters and grandees erected mansions on Legare Street and the Battery, so did other Charlestonians build their versions of home on the West Side, south of Line and north of Calhoun Street; the East Side, east of Rutledge and south of Line Street; and even on the lower peninsula, not just south of Calhoun but even in the sacred spaces south of Broad Street. These places were not inhabited by the white elite (though sometimes owned and built and rented out by them). The Charlestonians who lived in these cottages extend the boundaries of our knowledge of who made up the city; they show, among other things, that the color line was not as impermeable as some would have us believe. Black and white, high and low, rich and poor, all mixed together readily. In an era more integrated than ours, European immigrants and their children lived next door to people who had been born into slavery, or were descended from those African Americans who had been free. Their stories are just as interesting and just as necessary for us to get the city's full history.

These the author of this volume tells, and they are fascinating. Here are tales of rebellion—one house is on the site of that of free person of color Denmark Vesey, reputed to be a leader of a planned slave rebellion. There are human interest tidbits from the free people of color aristocracy, and there are more than mere hints of tragedy. There are suicides and losses of property to the tax man; the grim reaper appears too often on these streets, in the influenza pandemic, through malnutrition and in wasting diseases. There are so many children dying. But there are countless adoptions, too. People, poor as they are, are seen taking others in to share and make families. Lissa Felzer gives these modest homes great human and architectural interest; no snobbery of only the high born and high style is presented here. Within this book are those who have been left out of the Charleston story—bookbinders, drummers, masseuses, an African American United States Congressman and single mothers heading families. Sometimes their stories are not clear. They did not own much—they came and left the stage silently—but they were here. Their salt-of-the-earth lives offer the perfect antidote to our often too-treacly-sweet history.

If you cannot see their faces, you can glimpse their stories, and go see where they lived and dreamed. The tour will not take you to prominent East Bay or fashionable Legare, but to more modest and more real President and Line and Sheppard Streets, to Duc's Court and places long considered beyond the pale, beyond the boundaries and borders of what was important or even fit for polite company. We should be grateful to Lissa Felzer for documenting these lives and these buildings and returning them to us, acknowledged and seen. Doing this, she proves that Charleston history is more varied and dynamic and just more damned interesting than we had ever dreamed.

Harlan Greene
Avery Research Center for African American History and Culture
College of Charleston

ACKNOWLEDGEMENTS

This work took far longer than I would have ever imagined. Over the many years of research and writing, I had the encouragement, assistance and support of many people. I am afraid to list everyone out for fear of leaving anyone out, but I will give it my best shot! Thanks to my friends and family first—especially Greg—for all of your support in spite of the many late nights and much grumbling.

I cannot adequately express my appreciation to Harlan Greene for helping me puzzle out approaches to the most difficult aspects of my research, for working on my behalf while on vacation and for helping me stay on track when things got tough. I have always had a great deal of respect and admiration for you. Thanks for sharing some of what I admire so much about you.

I owe much gratitude to my MIL, Joanne Felzer, for reading and rereading draft after draft, and for fielding my constant barrage of thoughts, questions and research failures and successes.

Sarah Fick, Bob Stockton and Craig Bennett, thanks for sharing your brains with me and fielding questions. Bill Bowick and David Bouffard, thanks for all of your encouragement, and for your assistance with design elements. Mandi Herring Bello, all your love and care for my children made this go a whole lot faster than it otherwise would have! Amanda W. Franklin, thank you for your research assistance when I was running out of time. Tracy McKee, map-maker-extraordinaire, thank you for all of your efforts and hard work on my behalf. Holly Hobart, thanks for chauffeuring me around for photography early on. Thanks also to my College of Charleston students. Whether or not you are aware of this, you kept me enthusiastic about this book despite its slow progress.

Last but not least, I cannot forget to express my gratitude to those people who assisted me directly with my research. Everyone at the South Carolina History Room of the Charleston County Library has my gratitude for seemingly unlimited patience and assistance day after day: Nick Butler, Maryanne Cawley, Lish Thompson, Christina Shedlock, Molly French, Katie Gray and Liz Newcomb. I will miss seeing you all so regularly, but I am sure another project will take hold of me soon enough! And, of course, many thanks to Jenny Kaemmerlen, Lee Handford and Laura All at The History Press for your patience, assistance, pep talks/encouragement and for keeping me moving. I could not have gotten this done without the help of every one of you. I am very lucky to have such a vast group of friends and supporters! I hope you enjoy reading this as much as I enjoyed writing it.

I cannot forget Hannah B. Felzer, who laid at my feet to keep me company (and my feet warm) for every minute that I sat at my desk writing!

INTRODUCTION

.

The idea for this book was conceived around 2001 or 2002, while I was working for the City of Charleston as the senior preservation planner. I learned all of the folklore related to freedman's cottages and became fascinated with them. Charleston's freedman's cottages were then, and still are, one of the most understudied vernacular building types in the city. As is typical of written history, little is known about these buildings because no one "of note" is associated with them, with a few exceptions. The most predominant myth about these buildings is that they were constructed for and/or by freed slaves after the Civil War. In actuality, they were built for and occupied by the lower and middle classes of Charleston. These are the very citizens that made up the backbone of this city, or any city, for that matter. It is only in recent years that historians have begun to study more of the history of the lower and middle classes as it is through them that we can really understand the true history of our cities and country as a whole.

I could go on researching each building and every family that ever occupied each of these buildings—their stories never end. However, the intention of this work is to get some research done and circulate truthful information as opposed to the folklore, rumors and speculation that has been thrown around for years. It is by no means the end of the study, but rather the beginning, as I have only just touched on the subject here. This work focuses mainly on extant, relatively intact cottages. Through informal survey, I have identified about two hundred extant cottages. Generally speaking, sixty-three of those have been studied for this work, with forty-one of them being studied in depth and written about here. If all two hundred-plus buildings were to be studied before writing anything, this work would not be done for years, and I believe it is a story worth telling, or at least starting, now.

Research materials relied upon most heavily for this work include Charleston County and City ward books (tax records), Charleston City directories, property deeds and indices, Charleston County probate records, the Freedman's Bank Records, historical maps, plats and census records. Some of the research materials were self-limiting, creating a somewhat artificial time span of up until 1961 to study. After 1961, tax records are not kept in the same format, and the Charleston City directories no longer indicate the race of occupants of a house. Since much of this research is reliant upon demographic information, and I could no longer find out key information after 1961, I used that as an end date to researching the history of most of these structures. If the same family continued to reside in or own a particular structure after 1961, I followed them through their residence or ownership.

Another important avenue of research explored was oral history. Attempts were made to interview occupants; surviving family members of early occupants of these cottages; or long-term owners. Relatives and long-term residents were difficult, if not impossible, to find in most cases. Unfortunately, others identified were not always responsive.

While reading this work, it is important to keep in mind that the source for most of the provided years of birth was the United States Federal Census. Within the census records the month and year of birth are provided for some years, others just an age. Often the census records are in conflict with each other, and with other records, and therefore may not be entirely accurate. No census taker ever asked for proof of age! When the opportunity arose to check a date against a more reliable source such as a death or birth certificate, the opportunity was seized, and errors were corrected. These were rare opportunities.

When researching the ethnicity of an occupant, I relied on data found in the city directories and the census records. Some of the terms found there are somewhat archaic and do not have the same meaning today as they did then. Those terms were put in quotation marks.

When trying to determine if an African American was a "freed slave," I turned to the Freedman's Bank Records and capitation tax records for the City of Charleston as well as the State of South Carolina. If a person was born in South Carolina before the end of the Civil War, was an African American and did not appear in the capitation records, they were assumed to have been enslaved. However, there were limitations to this as well. The capitation records only provide a record for those individuals over the age of fifteen, so if a person was born in 1860, for instance, whether they were free or enslaved, they would not appear in these records. For additional information I checked the Freedman's Bank Records. If a person was listed in this source, that was also taken as proof of their previous enslavement.

All the photography was completed by me between the years 2000 and 2008. The architectural drawings were also completed by me. They are meant to be representative floor plans and not exact representations of any particular dwelling. They are compilations of surveys and architectural drawings found on file at the City of Charleston's Department of Planning, Preservation and Economic Innovation and the archives at Historic Charleston Foundation. The maps were created by Tracy McKee, director of the GIS Division for the City of Charleston (see the disclaimer at the end of this work).

An attempt has been made to find representative buildings for each geographic region of the peninsula—south of Calhoun Street; the west side, south of Line and north of Calhoun Street; the east side; and the upper peninsula. While some physical fabric has been studied for this book, the concentration is mainly on the social history of the buildings rather than the architectural history. I wanted to tell the story more of who lived in these tiny buildings rather than document the buildings themselves—that is another project in and of itself. In an effort to continue this research, I have set up a website and am asking for assistance. The website lists all of the extant cottages I have identified on the peninsula. I would welcome any historical information known regarding these buildings, as well as the locations of others. Please visit www.charlestoncottages.net for more information.

"FREEDMAN'S COTTAGE"
DEFINED

The term "freedman's cottage" relates to a building typology as opposed to who lived there or built it. In most cases, freedman's cottages are single-story wood-framed structures with a gable roof and a piazza (in Charleston, "piazza" refers to side porches found throughout the city) on the south or west side. The gable end is always oriented toward the street. This orientation is typical of Charleston's vernacular structures, a rhythm established by the long, narrow lots of the city. The plan of the building is generally one room wide and two rooms deep, with a central fireplace between the two rooms. Alternatively, there may be two exterior fireplaces, one for each room, on the north or east wall. Later adaptations of the plan may include three rooms in a linear fashion, or the rear of the piazza being built as enclosed space to house a bathroom or just additional interior space. The house is entered from one of two doors off the piazza—each room having its own entrance. The piazza itself is entered through a screen door that faces the street.

There are a few cottages that were constructed out of concrete in the early twentieth century as an alternative to the more traditional wood-frame structures. Those will be discussed in depth in a later chapter. This use of an alternative material for a traditional form speaks to the relative success of the building type.

Some believe that there are two types of freedman's cottages—the rectangular cottage and the L-shaped cottage. However, research indicates that the L-shaped cottage is nothing more than the traditional rectangular cottage with an addition to the south or west side of the building, followed often by a modification of the piazza so it too becomes L-shaped. Most often the addition was constructed very early in the life of the building and thus can be difficult to discern as an addition without careful analysis.

The Charleston "Freedman's Cottage"

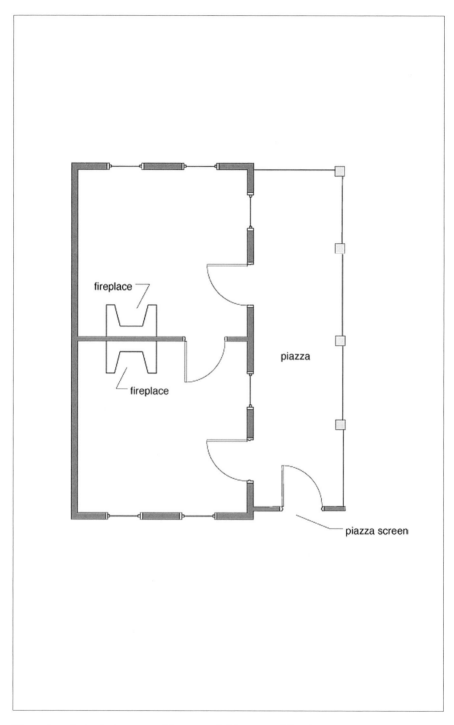

Floor plan of a typical cottage with a central chimney and fireplaces.

An Architectural Tradition

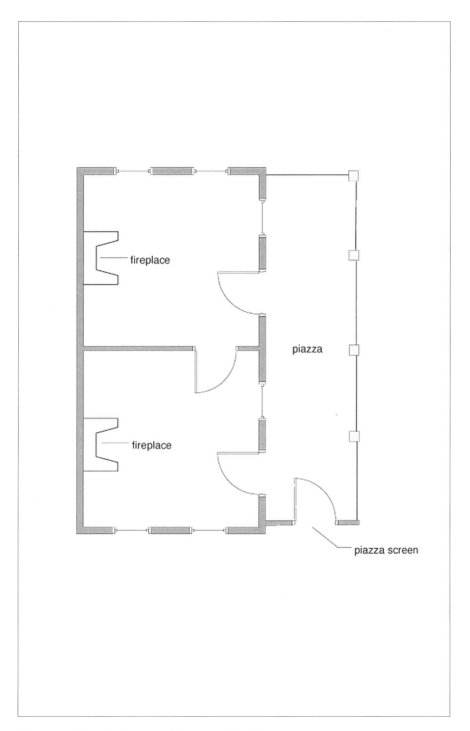

fireplace

piazza

fireplace

piazza screen

Floor plan of a typical cottage with two exterior chimneys.

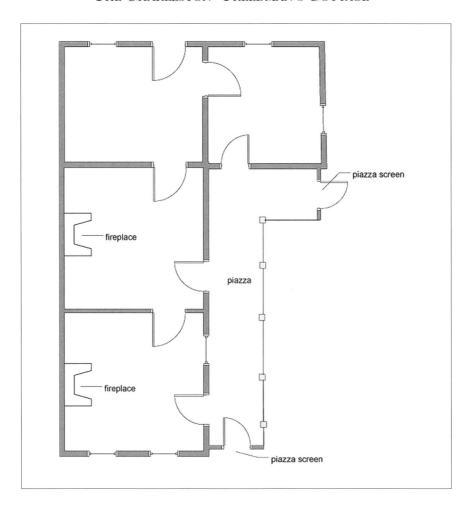

Floor plan of a typical "L-shaped" cottage.

The cottages were constructed very small, ranging between three hundred to five hundred square feet. Very few freedman's cottages remain without some sort of addition, either to the rear, the side, by filling in the piazza or some combination of all three. As previously stated, later cottages were often built with the rear of the piazza already enclosed to increase interior space and adaptability to modern living. Generally speaking, the original footprints of these houses, not including the piazza, are about twelve to fourteen feet wide and twenty-two to twenty-seven feet long. Most often, the piazza runs the full length of the house and is five to seven feet wide and proportional to the width of the main body of the house. Depending on when the house was constructed and by whom, the details such as piazza columns and balustrades, cornices and piazza screens vary, making each one unique and reflective of the builder's taste and/or stylistic trends of the time.

These buildings have often been compared to the long, narrow shotgun houses of New Orleans, or referred to as a single-story Charleston single house. The Charleston single house is a common vernacular building that is two rooms deep and one room wide in plan. They are typically two or three stories in height. Most Charleston single houses have a central stair hall, although smaller ones often do not. Additionally, they have a piazza on the south or west elevation that can be one to three stories in height depending on the size of the building itself. The freedman's cottage is a building type all of its own. It is not as deep as a shotgun house, and lacks some of the fundamental features of a Charleston single house, such as the central hall and staircase.

The majority of these cottages were constructed between 1880 and 1900, which may be explained by a booming economy, with 1883 being the best fiscal year the city had experienced since the Civil War. Between 1881 and 1885, over a thousand structures were erected north of Line, Cannon and Amherst Streets. Then in 1887, in the aftermath of the earthquake, the *News and Courier* reported that 6,956 residences were repaired or rebuilt, and 271 new buildings erected. Of those 271 new buildings, 51 were described as one-story wood structures. Of course not all of them were definitely freedman's cottages, but the majority of these structures were located in areas of the peninsula that contain large concentrations of this building type, and many have been verified to be freedman's cottages.

In addition to all the cottages that were constructed in these two decades, a handful were constructed before the Civil War, with the earliest one being 56 Bull Street, believed to be constructed circa 1830. The building type was evidently successful, as it continued to be constructed as late as 1925. To further punctuate their success, these cottages were the inspiration for a new 1990 residential design referred to as "Charleston Cottages." They were designed by a local architect, Chris Rose, working for Chris Schmitt and Associates, to house people making the transition from being homeless to renting on the open market. They received national attention and a merit award from the American Institute of Architects.

Freedman's cottages were constructed all over the Charleston peninsula, with highest extant concentration in the upper peninsula between Line and Mount Pleasant Streets. Several cottages were even constructed in North Charleston on upper Meeting Street in the 2800 block, and further north off of Spruill Avenue. Several of those cottages remain today. Generally speaking, the cottages were constructed in groups, in rows of two to six or

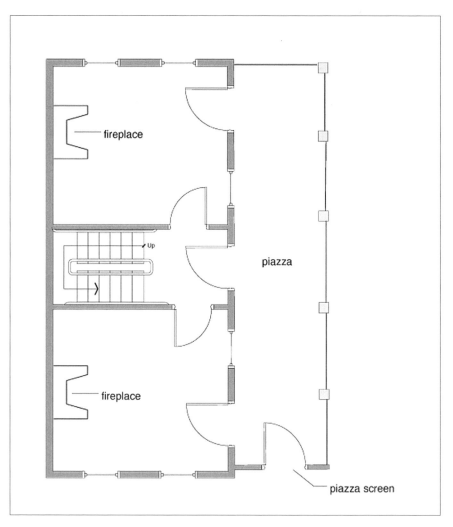

Floor plan of a typical Charleston single house.

more, or individually. In some instances (for example, on President Street), individual builders or property owners constructed the houses independent of each other in a row several years apart. The largest known group of freedman's cottages appeared on the east side of upper Meeting Street between Cool Blow Street and Cedar Street. The area was a portion of "Cool Blow Village," platted in 1884. There were twenty-eight of these cottages constructed on the lots by 1889. They were commissioned by Daniel O'Brien, an Irish immigrant born in 1844. In the 1920s and '30s, they became known as the "Eickmeyer Tenements," for owner William

Eickmeyer. The whole complex was demolished in the 1960s, presumably as part of urban renewal. The area sits vacant today.

The term "freedman's cottage" appears to be a very modern term. Some local historians believe the term originated in the 1970s, but cannot recall the context. It or some slight variation thereof, seems to have first appeared in writing in the late 1980s. For example, the "East Side Design Guidelines" written by Robert M. Leary and Associates for the City of Charleston in 1986 refers to 34 Sheppard Street as a "Freeman's House," and states that the name "may reflect the large number of free blacks who lived in the area prior to the Civil War." That statement indicates that the term likely had not been in use for long, given that the author was not sure what it was referencing.

From the late 1980s through the early 1990s the term had been used inconsistently. Notable historians and writers, when writing about specific cottages, failed to call them "freedman's cottages" but rather just likened them to one-story Charleston single houses. It was not until the late 1990s that the term was used consistently and referred only to a building type, with little regard to the actual history of the structure. As previously stated, in recent decades it was believed that freedman's cottages were built for and/or by freed slaves after the Civil War—this thought seems to prevail in some very recent writings. However, as more research is done, it is becoming clear that this is simply not the case. Because of this, local historians are now questioning whether or not the name of the buildings should change simply to the "Charleston cottage," which is the same name given to the cottages designed by Chris Rose in 1990.

PART I

THE LOWER PENINSULA

South of Calhoun Street

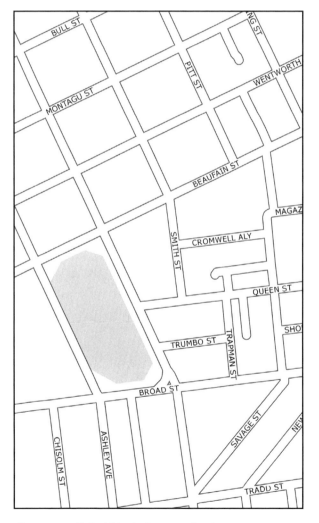

Cottages studied within the lower peninsula.

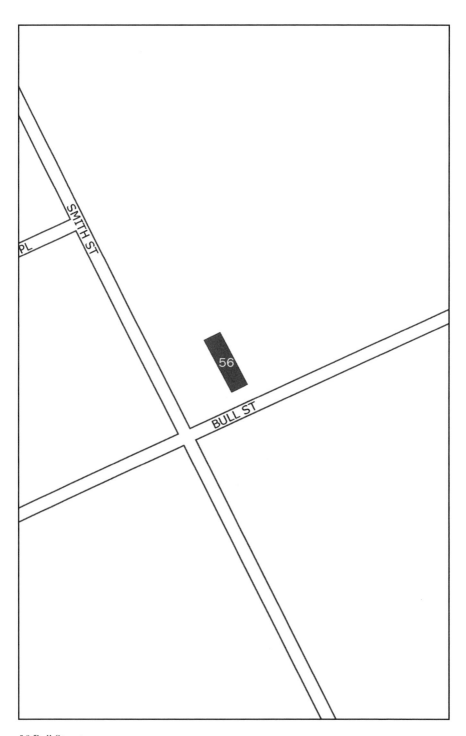

56 Bull Street.

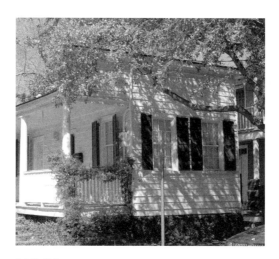

56 Bull Street.

56 Bull Street

This Greek Revival cottage is located on the north side of Bull Street, just east of Smith Street. Of all the extant freedman's cottages in the city of Charleston, this one is the oldest, having been constructed circa 1830. This house was once believed to be constructed and occupied by Denmark Vesey, leader of a thwarted slave insurrection of 1822. However, this theory was disproved in 1980. A thorough analysis of the building itself and some additional research into the history of the property and neighborhood was done in 1980 by the staff at South Carolina Department of Archives and History and a restoration consultant they hired. The restoration consultant looked at the construction methods used, and from that information was able to determine that the house could not have been constructed any earlier than 1830. Some of these construction method details included circular saw marks in all the wood elements and "modern" cut nails dating to 1830–40, particularly on the oldest portion (the front two rooms). The consultant did find a foundation for a fireplace under the piazza that predates the piers for the oldest part of the house. This would suggest an earlier building on the site. Whether or not this earlier building was actually Vesey's house is unknown.

With the circa-1830 construction date in mind, one of two people may have commissioned its construction: John Dougherty, who purchased the parcel in 1829, or John H. Seyle, who purchased it in 1835. Neither deed refers to this specific property but rather to a larger parcel (which would include this land area) at the corner of Smith and Bull Streets. Neither deed mentions any buildings, which is likely an error, as previous deeds and mortgages mention many buildings on that larger parcel. Genealogical information about either one of these men is difficult to find, but it is known that neither one ever occupied the house. As a matter of fact, it does not appear to ever have been owner-occupied.

From 1892 (when the address first appears in the city directories in the "Street Department") through 1945, the house was occupied solely by African American tenants in various occupations, such as a driver, a tailor, a shoemaker, a carpenter, a blacksmith, a cook, a laundress and a chauffer, to name a few. The average length of stay for any one family or individual until 1913 was about three years.

In 1913, members of one African American family, the Jones family, began renting the house and remained there through 1930. The first member of the family to occupy the house was James Jones, who worked as a plumber and was unmarried during the time he occupied the house. After Jones moved out, his two sisters, Theodosia and Rebecca, moved in. The sisters had been living together with another sister, Olive, since at least 1910. Between 1916 and 1930, Theodosia and/or Rebecca occupied 56 Bull Street. All of the sisters were born in South Carolina—Theodosia in 1883, Rebecca in 1886 and Olive in 1890. They all worked as laundresses from home or for private families. In 1920, Rebecca and Theodosia shared the house with their niece and nephew. After 1920, no records can be found for any members of the family except Theodosia. She remained in the house until 1930. She died in 1939, unmarried and without children. Documentation of the cause of her death cannot be found.

After the Jones family left the house, 56 Bull Street was again home to a series of short-term tenants, some being unemployed, single African American women and their children during WWII, and then later small families from the late 1940s through 1961. After 1945, the demographics of the neighborhood began to change, which is reflected in the occupants of the house. The occupants were low- to middle-income white families employed in such occupations as a truck driver and a shoe salesman.

Number 56 Bull Street has undergone many alterations throughout its long history, including two rear additions. The original building was a typical two-room cottage with a piazza on the west side. The middle section was constructed fairly early, but after 1840, and the rear square four-room addition is from the turn of the twentieth century. During the twentieth century, it has undergone multiple renovations without any apparent changes to the footprint.

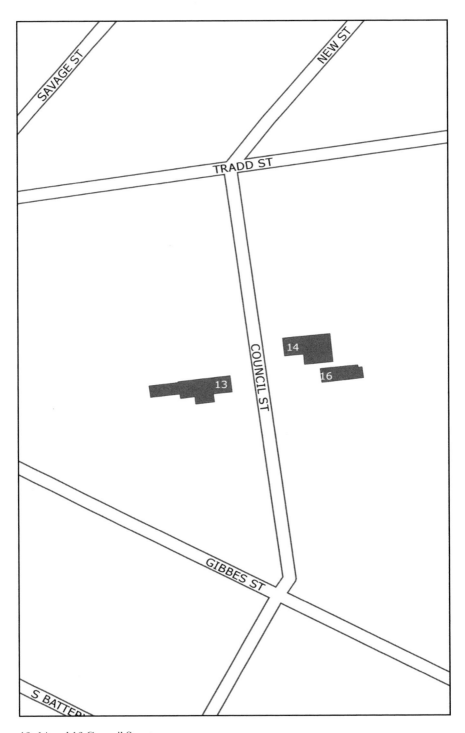

13, 14 and 16 Council Street.

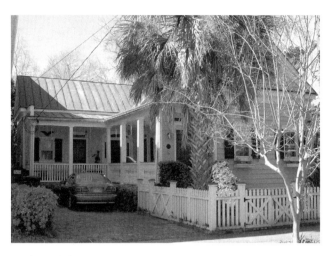

13 Council Street.

13 Council Street

The cottage at 13 Council Street is located on the west side of the street, between Tradd and Gibbes Streets. It was constructed in 1883 and commissioned by John Ahrens. It is possible that Ahrens even did the actual construction, since he worked as a contractor at least from 1907 through 1911. Ahrens purchased many parcels on Council Street in February 1883, in partnership with Samuel J.L. Matthews. In August of the same year, Ahrens and Matthews split their Council Street holdings. Whether or not the house was constructed at this point is unclear, but by 1884, the tax records indicate a "new house" on the lot. Interestingly enough, the earthquake damage report of 1886 also refers to this house as new.

Ahrens was born in Virginia in 1844 or 1845 to John and Mary Ahrens of Germany. Ahrens worked primarily as a merchant, selling dry goods and liquor, but as previously mentioned he also worked for a few years as a contractor, and had his office at 21 Council Street. Throughout much of the late nineteenth and early twentieth centuries, Ahrens resided at 1 New Street, but it is possible that for brief periods between 1886 and 1904 he lived in and/or worked at 13 Council.

Ahrens was married twice. His first wife was Annie or Anna. The exact date of their marriage is unknown, but they appear to have been married as early as 1870. There is no record of them having had any children, and Anna died of tuberculosis at the age of fifty-six on May 27, 1900. Only a year later, Ahrens married his second wife, Teresa C. Dillon, who was thirty-two years his junior. The second Mrs. Ahrens ran an additional store on Council Street prior to her husband's death. She sold "dry goods, notions, and fancy goods." Ahrens died on July 7, 1920, after an unspecified illness. Having had no children of his own in spite of two marriages, Ahrens bequeathed most of his estate to his wife, but also left money to two friends, a nephew, three nieces and two grand-nieces. Number 13 Council Street was then sold by his estate in 1921 to Henry H. Carter.

Henry H. Carter was born in 1895 to John and Minnie Carter. Carter's father worked in a cotton press or as a baker throughout his life. His mother was born in Germany and immigrated to South Carolina in 1885. In 1913, Carter married Pearl Elizabeth Breno, who was sixteen years his junior. Carter was employed by the U.S. Post Office as a letter carrier, beginning in 1913, and then as a clerk. The Carters moved into the house in 1922 with their toddler, Helen (b. 1920). In 1926, Pearl gave birth to another child, this time a son named for his grandfather, John.

Carter died in March 1927 from a self-inflicted gunshot wound to the head. He killed himself in the bathroom of the post office at the corner of Meeting and Broad Streets after a meeting with his supervisor. A rather graphic newspaper article described the incident: "The bullet fired from a .44 calibre Colt revolver entered his mouth and came out the top of his head and imbedded itself in the ceiling." His body was found by the janitor "lying in a pool of blood."

In August 1928, Pearl remarried another employee of the post office, Christian Redell. One year later, she gave birth to their daughter, Claire. Whether or not they had any additional children is unknown. Christian died in 1968, at the age of eighty-five, and Pearl in 1979, at the age of eighty. Pearl resided in the house until 1972, and transferred ownership of the property to her children in 1977.

Number 13 Council Street appears in an "L" shape as early as 1920. The overall footprint of the building changed so much over time that it is difficult to discern its original configuration, but is assumed to be the typical two-room cottage with a piazza based on physical fabric. The most recent known alteration to the footprint is a rear addition completed in 1996.

14 and 16 Council Street, the Graddicks

Numbers 14 and 16 Council Street are located on the east side of the street, directly across from 13 Council. In 1876, Henry T. Graddick purchased the land where 14 and 16 Council Street sit from Henry M. Holmes. Sometime before 1883, he subdivided the lots and sold 16 Council to Henry Lester Graddick. The house at 16 Council was constructed in 1883, and 14 Council was constructed in 1886. In the years prior to construction, both men lived at 10 Council Street, a two-story single house that they had built as well, or next door to each other in other houses on Council Street. Henry T. moved into 14 Council in 1887, and lived there through 1894. At that time, Henry L. moved to 99 Coming Street with his family and lived out the remainder of his life there.

The genealogy of this family is somewhat confusing as records are scant and occasionally conflicting. Throughout the 1870s and 1880s, Henry T., Henry L. and Frank Graddick lived on Council Street, either in one house or next door to each other. All three men were "mulatto" mariners referred to as "Captain." Frank and Henry L. were brothers, with their father being Henry T. Their location on Council Street was likely for convenience, given that there was a shipyard at the end of the street in the late nineteenth and early twentieth centuries.

Henry T. was born in 1815 in South Carolina, and was likely born free. Only five years after he was born, a law was passed making freeing a slave nearly impossible. The law stated that slaves could only be freed through

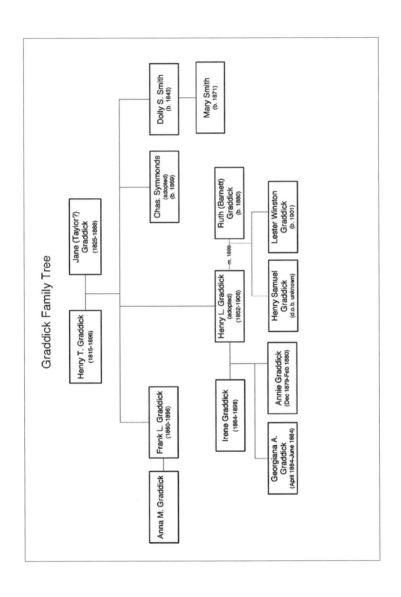

Graddick Family Tree

Henry T. Graddick (1815-1896)

Jane (Taylor?) Graddick (1825-1888)

Dolly S. Smith (b. 1843)

Mary Smith (b. 1871)

Chas. Symmonds (adopted) (b. 1869)

Frank L. Graddick (1860-1896)

Anna M. Graddick

Henry L. Graddick (adopted) (1852-1905)

— m. 1899 —

Ruth (Barnett) Graddick (b. 1880)

Lester Winston Graddick (b. 1901)

Henry Samuel Graddick (d.o.b. unknown)

Irene Graddick (1864-1898)

Annie Graddick (Dec 1879-Feb 1880)

Georgiana A. Graddick (April 1884-June 1884)

approval of state legislation. This was in response to some slaveholders who freed troublesome, old or sickly slaves who then became burdens on the community. The law required the approval by a commission for any future manumission (act of freeing a slave).

Additionally, South Carolina state law required that all free persons of color had to pay a capitation tax (fixed tax per person as opposed to an income tax) to retain their freedom. It was a way to monitor the whereabouts of free people of color and to ensure that no escaped slaves were posing as free blacks.

Henry T. was married to Jane (Taylor?), who was eleven years his junior. The date of their marriage is unknown, but they were married by 1850, and listed as "free inhabitants" of the city of the Charleston. They had several children through birth or adoption: Henry L., adopted (b. 1856), Frank L. (b. 1860), Dolly S. (b. 1843) and Charles Symmonds, adopted (b. 1869). The 1880 census records indicate that Dolly, her daughter, Mary, and Charles were living with them at 14 Council Street. Mrs. Graddick died of "Chronic Hemorrhages" related to tuberculosis at 14 Council Street in 1888. Henry T. died in 1896, and no record can be found as to the cause of his death.

As previously stated, Henry Lester Graddick was born in 1856, yet the place of his birth is unknown due to conflicting records. Some indicate Texas while others indicate South Carolina. The death certificate of his brother, Frank, states that Frank was born in Haiti and arrived in Charleston in 1866. Depending on when the family returned from Haiti to South Carolina, it is possible that Henry Lester was born in Haiti as well.

Prior to the Civil War, the government of Haiti actively encouraged free African Americans to immigrate to Haiti. Immigrants were promised a homestead and tools for working the land. They were also promised room and board from the time they arrived until they could get settled. For some, however, they had a hard time getting the Haitian government to deliver on these promises once they arrived.

Henry L. was married twice and had several children. His first wife was Irene, born in 1864. The length of their marriage is unknown, but at least one infant daughter died of "Marasmus" (severe malnutrition) and one was still-born while the family lived on Council Street. Irene died in the state hospital in Columbia of tuberculosis at the age of thirty-four in 1898. Graddick's second wife was Ruth Weston Barnett. They married in June 1899, and had two sons, Henry Samuel and Lester Winston. When Graddick died in 1906, his will specified that his estate be divided in thirds between his wife and sons, but no inventory was done so it is impossible to tell what he owned specifically besides the property at 99 Coming Street. Frank Graddick is not found in any of the United States census records, but it is known that he did die in the city of Charleston in 1896. Very little information beyond that can be found about him.

There were three vessels listed in the records that the Graddick men captained: a schooner *Robert E. Lee*, a schooner *Minnie Ha Ha* and a sloop *Ellen*. When Frank died in 1896, his widow sold the *Minnie Ha Ha* and the *Robert E. Lee* to his brother Henry L. Ownership of the *Ellen* is unclear as it is not mentioned in any estate records. Interestingly enough, the parents of DuBose Heyward, well-known author of the novel *Porgy* (later adapted to the opera *Porgy and Bess*), were friends of Henry Lester, who used to loan them his schooner, the *Robert E. Lee*, so they could go sailing when DuBose was a child.

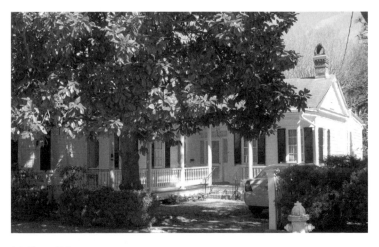

14 Council Street.

14 Council Street

As previously stated, 14 Council Street was constructed in 1886 and was occupied by Henry T. Graddick for the first seven years after construction. After Graddick left the house in 1895, he maintained ownership and rented out the house until it was sold by his estate in 1898. The property was then purchased by George Anthony Simonin, a "pressman" for the *News and Courier*. Simonin owned and occupied the house with his family through 1930. Simonin was born in 1862 in South Carolina to George and

Anne Simonin. His father was a policeman, born in South Carolina, and his mother emigrated from France. Simonin married Mary France Flatlay in 1884—Flatlay arrived in the United States from Ireland in 1873. Mary worked at the navy yard as a telephone operator as early as 1908, and remained employed there until she died. The Simonins had ten children, four daughters and six sons, all born between 1886 and 1907. In 1900, there were two adults and eight children ranging in age from eight months to fourteen years all living in this small cottage on Council Street! Mary Simonin died in the house at the age of sixty-two in 1930. After she died, George went to live in West Palm Beach with one of his children and died in 1939. Upon his death, the property was willed to two of his sons, Leo and Charles, but was sold by his estate in 1940.

During the 1930s, the house was occupied by three separate families, who stayed for a year or two only. They were employed by such organizations as an amusement park, an insurance agency and the United States Coast Guard. In 1940, Marguerite Wood, clerk and stenographer for a U.S. district attorney's office, purchased the property from Simonin's estate and by 1942, she and her family were living in the house. The property remains in the Wood family's possession. With the exception of the Graddicks, 14 Council Street has been owned and occupied by white families throughout its history.

Number 14 Council Street is an L-shaped cottage modified as such before 1902. A rear addition with a shed roof was constructed and a bay was added to the front façade. Both of these modifications do not appear on any maps through 1944.

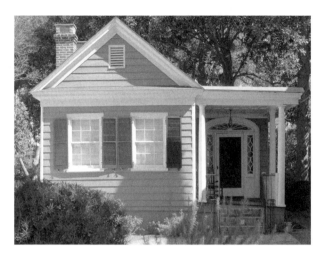

16 Council Street.

16 Council Street

The cottage at 16 Council Street has a more diverse history than its neighbor. From its construction in 1883 through the 1960s, the house has only been owner-occupied sporadically. The first known occupants were Matthew Eugene Slavish and his family, who occupied the house from 1888 through 1891. Slavish was born in South Carolina in 1856 to immigrant parents (of Austria and England). He followed in his father's footsteps to become a sea captain. Some sources report that he was also a carpenter. He married Mary E. Dunn in Charleston County in 1911. There is no evidence that they had any children together, but Mary brought one daughter with her from a previous marriage. Slavish died in 1931.

For a brief period in the 1910s, the property was held as an investment by well-known Charleston preservationist and real estate agent, Susan Pringle Frost. In 1919, it was purchased and occupied by Mrs. Flora LaBruce, an artist and president of Carolina Arts and Crafts, Inc. Mrs. LaBruce sold the parcel the following year to a sales clerk, Thomas C. Welch. Welch occupied the house for about three years before renting it out to a co-worker. It was owner-occupied again in the 1950s and '60s when Virginia Johnston, secretary for the office of a U.S. district court judge, lived in the house.

Primarily, 16 Council Street was occupied by white individuals and families. Occupations ranged from skilled laborers such as carpenters and a well-borer, to clerks in department stores, to an engineer. No one person occupied the house for more than a few years in its early history. From 1907 until the house was purchased by Mrs. LaBruce, 16 Council Street was home to lower-income African Americans who were employed as hucksters, laborers, watchmen and carpenters.

Number 16 Council Street is a rectangular cottage that is set back from the street. It underwent many alterations and rear additions throughout its history. The configuration of the piazza was changed to include infill of a large portion early in its history. Later additional space on the piazza was enclosed, the piazza screen was removed and a Colonial Revival door surround was created at the entrance. In 1990, an application was made for the demolition of a "non-historic" rear addition, followed by the construction of a new single-story addition at the rear. Whether or not this work was completed is unknown.

PART II

THE WEST SIDE

South of Line Street and North of Calhoun Street

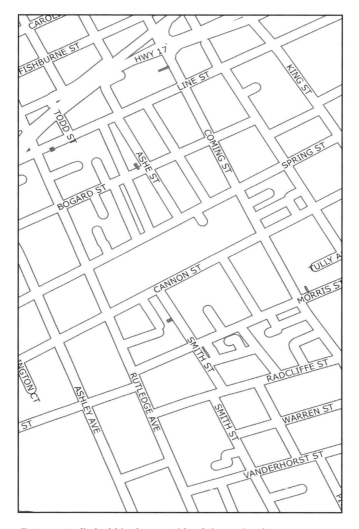

Cottages studied within the west side of the peninsula.

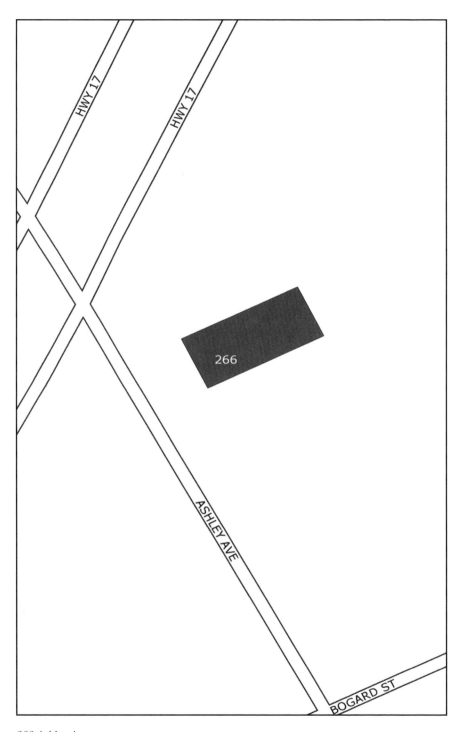

266 Ashley Avenue.

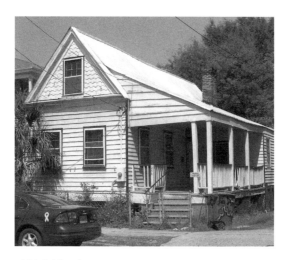

266 Ashley Avenue.

266 ASHLEY AVENUE

The building located at 266 Ashley Avenue (formerly Ashley Street) is a one-and-one-half-story cottage located on the east side of Ashley Avenue, just south of the Crosstown Expressway. Records indicate that a building was constructed on the lot between 1896 and 1898. The construction was commissioned by Prince G. Anderson after he purchased the property in 1896. This parcel is one of 101 lots that were created in 1892 from a subdivision of Horsey's Farm, which was subdivided by Henry Haesloop.

Anderson lived in the house for a short period of time prior to converting it to rental property. It was not owner-occupied again until Anderson's estate was settled in 1917, at which time the property was purchased by the person renting it, Daniel A. Bythewood. Bythewood sold the property in 1928, after which the property changed hands only twice more prior to being sold to the current owner. It was used as investment property through at least the middle of the twentieth century.

Prince G. Anderson, who commissioned the construction of 266 Ashley Avenue, was an African American born in March 1857. Given that Anderson was so young in slavery times, if he was free he would not have appeared in the capitation records, so it is impossible to know if he was a former slave or not. The U.S. Federal Census records indicate that Anderson was a servant to a white family in 1870. By 1880, he was employed as a baker and was married to his first wife, Rebecca, a dressmaker. At that time, they had an unnamed four-month-old daughter. By 1898, Anderson was living at 266 Ashley Avenue. He continued to work as a baker, but was married to Hattie (Henrietta), a seamstress, to whom he had been married for four years. No records can be found to indicate what happened to his first wife. The 1900 census indicates that Prince and Hattie had a five-year-old son, Ulysses. Also living in the house were his two daughters Mattie (b.1880) and Nettie (b.1892) Mayrant. Presumably these daughters were from his previous marriage, Mattie being the unnamed four-month-old from the 1880 census. Hattie died at the young age of forty-three from an unspecified form of cancer. She died in the house on May 21, 1901. As early as 1903, the house was being used as investment property and Prince Anderson no longer resided there.

Prince Anderson died May 31, 1907. The cause of death is listed as "Morbus Brightii Uremia" (blood poisoning brought on by kidney failure). The dynamics of his family are puzzling. Anderson wrote his will about two weeks prior to his death and left out many members of his family. He bequeathed cash to Ulysses Benjamin Anderson and Ruth Anderson. The rest of his estate was to be divided between one Helen Duncan and Royal G. Anderson, relationship unknown. There is no mention of any of the other members of his family in the will, but it did take ten years to settle the estate.

Daniel A. Bythewood, also African American, began renting the property as early as 1907, and continued to do so until 1917, when he purchased the property from the estate of Prince Anderson. Bythewood was born in 1867 in South Carolina and worked as a carpenter. By 1910, he had a fairly large family, which consisted of his wife, Geneva (Perry), who he married in 1898, and four children, all living at 266 Ashley along with a boarder. By 1920, they had a total of five children living in the house, three sons and two daughters ranging in age from fourteen months to nineteen years. In 1928, they sold the property to R.F. Momeier and by 1930 had relocated to New York.

R.F. Momeier only held the property for a few months before selling it to Rosa T. Perry, Geneva's sister-in-law. The U.S. Federal Census records vary in their description of the race of this family. They are alternately listed as "mulatto" and "black," depending on the year. Rosa is consistently listed as a dressmaker or seamstress, and resided at 23 Percy Street with her extended family throughout most of her life. In the 1920 U.S. Federal Census, she was married to Christopher Perry, who was employed by the postal service as a letter carrier. By 1930, Rosa was a widow, and continued to reside at 23 Percy Street with her parents. There is no evidence of the Perrys ever having any children. In 1960, the property changed hands again when it was sold to St. Julian Matthews. Victoria Matthews, presumably St. Julian's widow, resided in the house until the late 1970s. At that point, the lot reverted to rental property and was occupied by a variety of individuals, such as a licensed practical nurse and various students.

The house at 266 Ashley Avenue is a one-and-one-half-story cottage similar to a freedman's cottage in form. It is one room wide and has a piazza on the south side, but it is three rooms deep as opposed to two. It is possible that it was originally constructed as a single-story dwelling, and later modified to suit the needs of the Bythewoods' large family. Since Daniel Bythewood was a carpenter, he would have been capable of making the modifications to the house while living there. These modifications may have included adding a central staircase, and either converting the attic to living space and adding a large dormer on the north side, or replacing the roof structure entirely to accommodate the extra living space in the attic story. However, an analysis of the material finishes was completed and has done little to support or negate these thoughts. Further investigation of the framing would need to be completed to understand the exact sequence of events regarding any subsequent alterations since the house's construction. However, given the three-room configuration and the fact that the ward books call this a two-story structure since it was constructed, it is likely that the upper half story is original to the house.

Early modifications were made to the footprint of the house. According to the physical fabric and the *Sanborn Fire Insurance Maps of the City of Charleston*, a small rear addition was constructed and the rear portion of the piazza was filled in prior to 1902. The rear addition was either encased in or completely replaced by a 1950s addition that was removed in 2006. The rear portion of the piazza remains enclosed, and this room also houses a small fireplace. The mortar analysis of the two fireplaces in the rear of the structure indicates that they were constructed at the same time, suggesting that the piazza infill is original. However, the physical fabric of the building indicates that the rear portion of the piazza was filled in after construction. The materials of the floor and ceiling in the rear room match those of the piazza. Given this information, it would seem that the piazza was enclosed and the fireplace added very early in the life of the house. Perhaps this fireplace was constructed with materials left over from the construction of the other fireplaces.

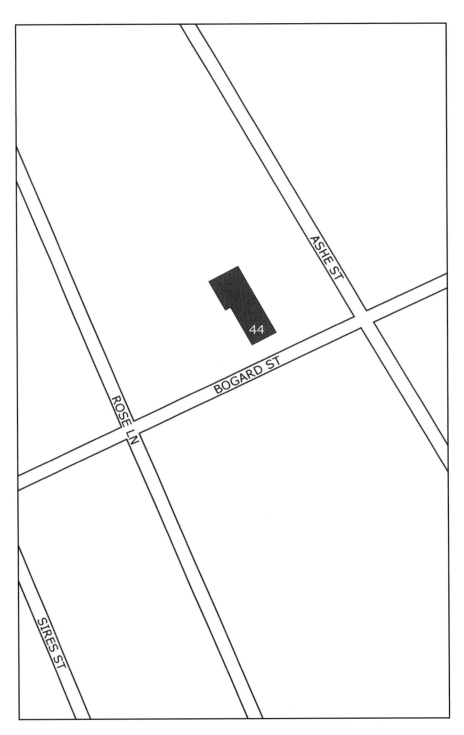

ASHE ST

BOGARD ST

ROSE LN

SIRES ST

44

44 Bogard Street.

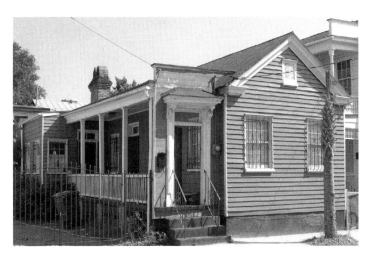

44 Bogard Street.

44 BOGARD STREET

Number 44 Bogard Street is located on the north side of the street between Ashe Street and Rose Lane. Construction of the house was commissioned by Thomas W. Poinsette, an African American baker. Poinsette purchased the property in 1900 from a well-known developer and politician, Tristram Tupper Hyde. Hyde owned a prominent real estate and insurance business in Charleston. He was involved in the development of Hampton Park Terrace as well as the Rose Garden neighborhood in the upper peninsula. He was also elected mayor of Charleston in 1915. He ran for three terms, but was only elected to one. He was defeated by John P. Grace in the highly charged election preceding that one and the one following.

Poinsette obtained a mortgage from Progressive Building and Loan Association the same year that he purchased the property, presumably to finance construction. He occupied the house with his wife, Sarah, for less than three years until they sold the property to Eva Koofman in November 1903. The Poinsettes were married in 1887. Where they met, and the location of their marriage, is unknown. They were both born in South Carolina. Thomas was born in 1864 and Sarah in 1865 or 1866. There is no evidence that they ever had any children. After they sold 44 Bogard Street, they relocated to Los Angeles, California, where Poinsette opened his own bakery. He died in California in 1941.

Eva Koofman used the property as an investment and only held it until October 1905 before selling it to John J. Healy. Healy was a police officer for the City of Charleston, in which capacity he worked for most of his life, if not all. Healy was born in South Carolina in 1876 to Irish immigrant parents. In 1906, he married Helen A. Boyles, also born in South Carolina in 1877. The Healys never had any children. They invested heavily in the neighborhood, and by the time of Healy's death in 1937, they owned seven parcels on Bogard Street and two on St. Philip Street. Healy's entire estate was left to his sister-in-law, Margaret Boyles, as his wife predeceased him in 1931.

In 1921, the Healys moved across the street to 43 Bogard. Number 44 Bogard Street was then occupied by renters until it was purchased by the Hightowers in 1956. After the Healys moved out, several of the tenants worked for the Charleston Police Department or the City of Charleston. Detective Chauffeur Perry M. Fox and his wife occupied the house in 1927 and 1928. In 1929, John C. Addison and his wife, Louise (Gervais), moved into the house. Addison was a detective with the Charleston Police Department and his wife worked as a nurse. The Addisons were married in 1913 in Charleston. Mrs. Addison was previously married and had one son, Charles Aimar, born in 1904. There is no evidence that the Addisons had any additional children. The family remained in the house through 1938.

During the time the Hightowers owned the property, starting in 1956, a member of their family occupied the house through the year 2000. After the Hightowers sold the property, it changed hands three more times before being purchased by the current owner in 2005. Generally speaking, this house has been occupied by a mix of owners and tenants throughout its history. Thomas W. Poinsette was one of only two African American owners or tenants in the house through the year 2000.

The footprint of this house was altered very early in its history with a shed addition to the rear of the west side of before 1902. There was also a small addition constructed beyond that before 1902 as well. At some point during the twentieth century, another larger addition was constructed at the rear, completely engulfing or obliterating the second small early addition. Records indicate that the only other changes are related to several interior and exterior renovations that have occurred in the last ten years without changing the building envelope.

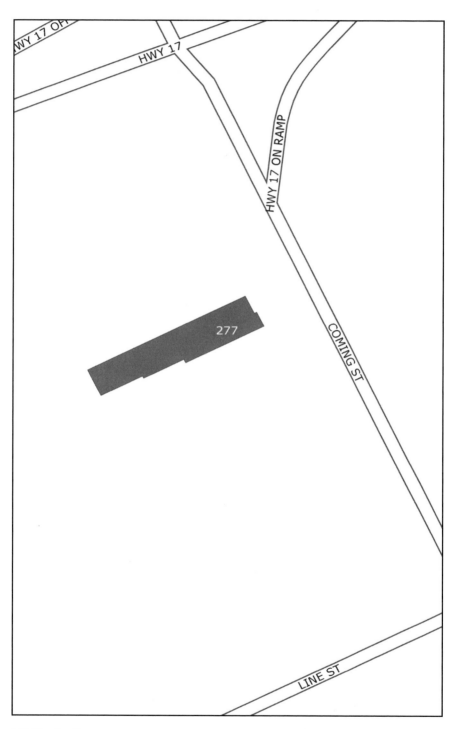

277 Coming Street.

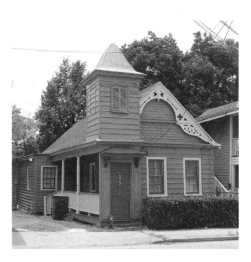

277 Coming Street.

277 COMING STREET

This Queen Anne cottage is located on the west side of Coming Street, north of Line Street and south of U.S. Highway 17. Construction of the building was commissioned by Robert W. Turner in 1875. He purchased the lot from the estate of John B. Mathewes in 1867. Turner was a "mulatto" born in Carolina County, Virginia, in 1830. Records indicate he was residing in Charleston by 1866 with his wife, Mary Ann (Matthews), and four daughters—Ada, Anne, Jane and Julia. Turner worked in various professions while living in Charleston, but primarily he was a merchant or grocer, selling "fruits and confectionary" prior to serving in the South Carolina House of Representatives from November 1872 through March 1874.

Turner and his family never lived at 277 Coming Street, but used the property as an investment. They resided instead above his shop on Calhoun Street. Turner held the property until his death in 1886, when he died from "rheumatism and laryngitis" at the age of sixty-one. His wife and daughters sold the property in 1891 to the tenant residing in the building at the time, Benjamin Moses Jones.

Jones was a previously enslaved African American gardener born in Charleston in 1829. He was born to Samuel and Celia Jones and was one of eight children. By 1870, he was married to Sintilla and had six children—Charles, James, Mary Jane, Elizabeth, Rosa and Henry. In 1869 and 1870, the Jones family resided at 40 Morris Street—another freedman's cottage studied for this work. They were not listed in the city directories in the 1860s and '70s so it is impossible to know where else they lived and for how long. By 1880, he was a widower, living with only three of his daughters at 153 Calhoun Street. Jones and his daughters only lived at 277 Coming Street from 1890 through 1894. As previously stated, Jones purchased the property in 1891 with a mortgage he obtained for $1,200 from Moses E. Lopez. In 1894, Jones defaulted on his loan and the parcel reverted to Lopez. During that same year, Lopez sold the parcel to John G.R. Richter.

John and Mary Richter never occupied the house, but rather occupied 138½ Line Street with six of their eight children. Richter was born in Alabama in March 1853 to German parents; his wife Mary (Isabel Bryan) was born in South Carolina in 1858. The Richter family seems to have had strong roots in Charleston, as the 1900 census indicates that this family, while living on Line Street, was living adjacent to "Richter's Court."

John Richter's life ended in 1902 at the age of forty-nine. He died in the state hospital in Columbia from "exhaustion from general paralysis," a perplexing diagnosis to say the least. Upon his death, his widow was left with five of their eight children still minors. Richter died intestate so the property transferred to his wife and the children after his death. In 1906, the three oldest children gave their interest in the property to their mother to aid in the support of the five youngest children. Mrs. Richter died in 1940. Her estate was divided up among her children and grandchildren according to a will. One year after her death, Mrs. Richter's daughter, Lottie I. Mappus, was declared "of unsound mind" and the property was sold at auction.

Between 1895 and 1917, the house was occupied by a variety of tenants who lived in the house only for a year or two at a time. They were a fairly even mix of white and African American, and worked in a number of trades, such as laborers, a train conductor, a bricklayer and a painter—curiously, a woman by the name of Annie Wright worked from the house as a "masseuse" in 1905.

In 1918, Rexford L. Richter moved into the house with his wife Artimisha (Curtis) and their two sons, Rexford and Lawrence. Richter was the youngest son of John and Mary Richter, born in August 1891. Richter worked as a driver for Ideal Laundry for many years, then as their "solicitor" (i.e. he solicited business for them) and finally as a sheet metal worker by 1930. He and his family resided in the house through 1926, when presumably they outgrew the tiny structure. By 1926, they had five children, lost one to "convulsions," and one more on the way. At that point, they moved into the house next door to Richter's mother on Line Street, and by 1930 they had six children, five sons and a daughter ranging in age from fifteen to three.

An Architectural Tradition

After the Richters moved out of the house, it again reverted to rental property and was subsequently occupied by a mix of white and African American unskilled workers until 1936. At this point, Thomas and Josephine (Boswell) Meree moved in. Thomas Meree was born to Thomas and Annie Meree of Charleston in 1894. Meree's father was a conductor for Southern Railway, for which company the younger Thomas was employed also as an adult. Thomas and Josephine were married in 1931 in Charleston County. They rented 277 Coming Street for ten years before purchasing the property in 1946. The family remained in the house with four to six of their children through at least 1961. The property changed hands four times between 1964 and 2000, when the current owners purchased it.

The footprint of this unique cottage has been extended with at least one rear addition in the mid-twentieth century, and the rear of the piazza was filled in. The fireplaces and chimneys have been removed, and in the year 2000 the cottage was gutted and extensively renovated.

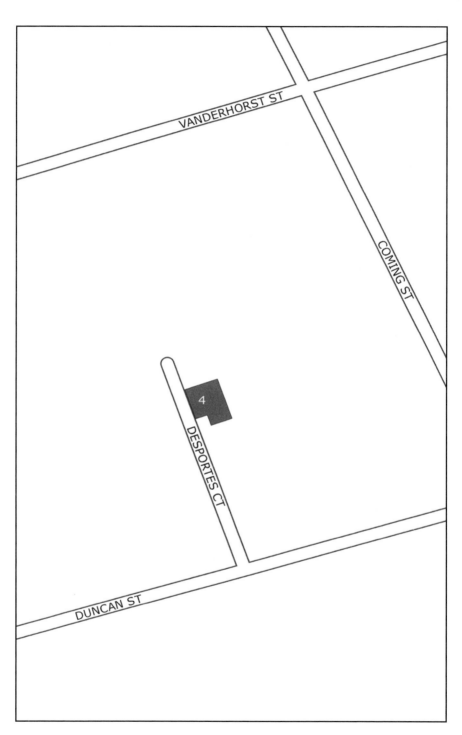

Map showing the location of 4–6 Desportes Court.

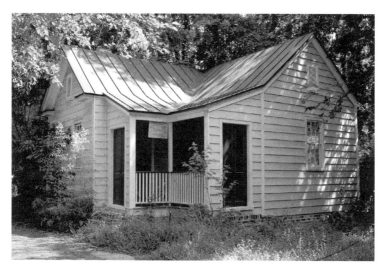

4–6 Desportes Court.

4–6 Desportes Court

Number 4–6 Desportes Court is a unique L-shaped cottage located on the east side of the street, constructed in 1892. It is unique in that the portions of the structure are equidistant, as opposed to most, if not all, of the other L-shaped cottages, which have one portion being longer than the other. Previous to this house, there was a two-story wooden structure on the lot that, according to the tax records, burned in October 1891. The two-story structure was rectangular in footprint, as was this building originally. Construction of this cottage was commissioned by Morris Charles Edwards, who purchased the property in 1881. The deed states that he purchased the property from a group of five "co-tenants." Edwards was a previously enslaved African American, born in Charleston in 1839. He was born to Morris and Louisa Edwards, and had three sisters and one brother. By 1869, he was living on Desportes Court—but the exact address is unknown. He was employed by the Citadel to "waite on Colonel Nichols." By 1881, he was working as a porter. In 1888, he married Josephine Blake. There is no record of them having any children. Morris and Josephine Edwards occupied the property until his death. He died in the house of "consumption and exhaustion" (tuberculosis) in July 1898. Mrs. Edwards remained in the house and worked as a seamstress until she lost the property at auction for unpaid taxes of $23.53 in October 1899. The property changed hands five more times before being purchased by the current owner in 1995.

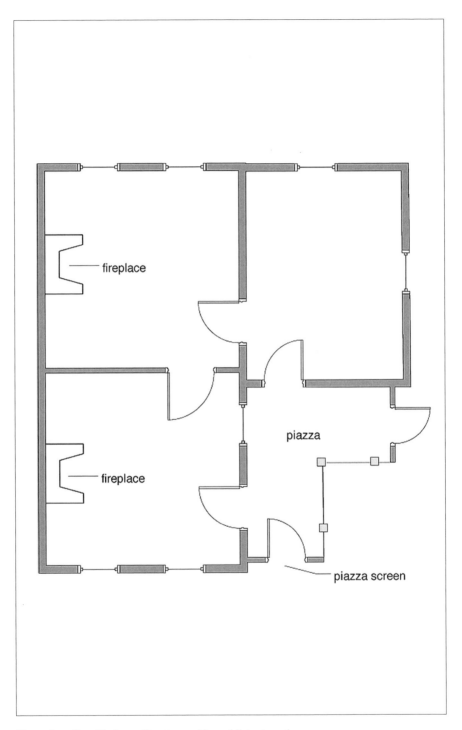

Floor plan of an "L-shaped" cottage with equidistant portions.

An Architectural Tradition

Although the records are scanty, it seems that the house was generally used for investment and occupied by low-income African American individuals and families employed as laborers, maids, laundresses and seamstresses throughout the first half of the twentieth century. None of the occupants remained in the house for more than a year or two. In 1956, the property was purchased by the tenants in the house at the time, Clement and Evelyn Brown. The Brown family, who had at least five children, occupied the house through 1995.

Number 4–6 Desportes Court was originally constructed as a rectangular two-room cottage with a piazza on the south side. Sometime between 1893 and 1902, a third room was added to the south side of the building and the piazza was modified, creating the L shape. Later the piazza was filled in to create more interior space. When it was purchased by the current owners in 1995, the building was uninhabitable due to fire damage. The current owners stabilized and repaired the cottage in 2001, but as of this writing it remains uninhabited.

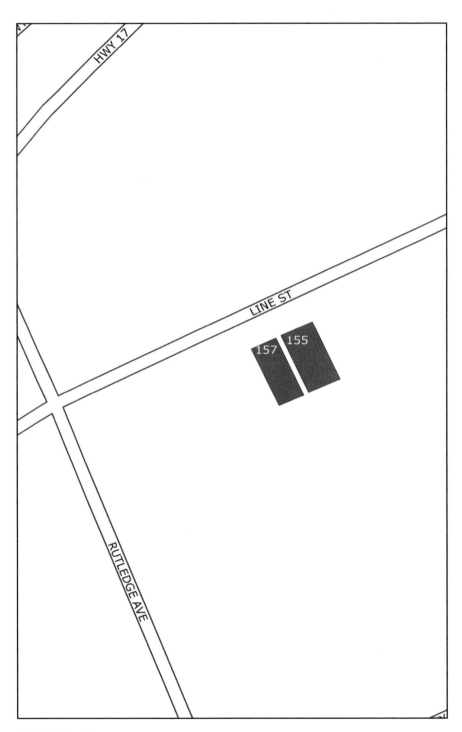

155–157 Line Street.

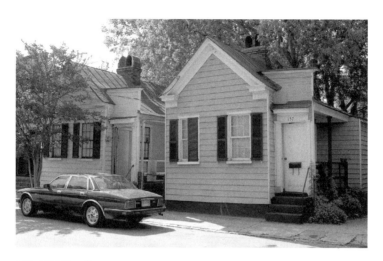

155–157 Line Street.

155 AND 157 LINE STREET

Numbers 155 and 157 Line Street are two cottages located on the south side of Line Street, just east of Rutledge Avenue, behind 270 Rutledge Avenue. They were constructed by 1890, and commissioned by Adolph Frederick Diedrick Hollings and his wife, Anna Rebecca Dorthea. Adolph and Anna Hollings were born in 1853 and 1849, respectively. Adolph Hollings was born in South Carolina, and Mrs. Hollings emigrated from Germany in 1866. They had five children, three daughters and two sons, and were the grandparents of former United States Senator Ernest F. Hollings. The Hollings family owned property at the intersection of Rutledge Avenue and Line Street since 1853, when Adolph Hollings's father, Behrend Henry Hollings, began purchasing property on the northeast corner. Eventually he established a grocery store on the northeast corner, which Adolph Hollings took over in 1865 when his father died. In 1885, Adolph Hollings purchased the lot at the southeast corner of Rutledge and Line. In just a few years, he transferred the property into his wife's name and the two freedman's cottages were constructed.

The first occupants of the houses were Kate Haffler, a white widow, at 155, and William Nesbit, an African American carpenter, at 157. There are no known records of who did the actual construction, but given that Nesbit was a carpenter, he may have been involved. Nesbit resided in the house through 1895, and Mrs. Haffler through 1896. For the most part, both houses were primarily occupied by African Americans, who were employed as laborers, blacksmiths, factory workers and maids. Mrs. Haffler was the only white occupant of 155 Line Street through 1961. The tenants only stayed in the houses for three to four years, with a few exceptions after 1920.

Andrew J. Campbell and his wife Mary resided at 155 Line Street from 1919 until 1927. Campbell worked at the cotton factory as a cotton sampler. No occupation is known for Mrs. Campbell. The 1920 census lists them as "mulatto" with no children. They were both born in South Carolina. Andrew Campbell was born in 1879, and his wife in 1890. Another long-term resident of 155 Line Street was African American Anna H. Rose. Little is known about Ms. Rose other than she lived in the house from 1940 through 1958, and worked as a maid.

Josephine White lived at 157 Line Street from 1922 through 1932. Ms. White was an African American born in South Carolina around 1888. In the 1920 census, she was listed as being married to Isaiah White, who worked in the cotton factory as a packer, but she was a widow by 1930. No other information can be found. Another long-term resident of 157 Line Street was Adeline Washington. Ms. Washington was born in South Carolina in 1891. She was raised in the Hollings household and was employed by them as a laundress. She lived at 157 Line Street from 1948 through the 1960s. The property remained in possession of the Hollings family until 1999.

These two houses are likely the smallest cottages studied for this book. Both structures have been added on to at the rear and had the rear of the piazza enclosed early in the twentieth century. Both buildings were extensively renovated in 2004. Despite these changes, these cottages retain their original charm and character.

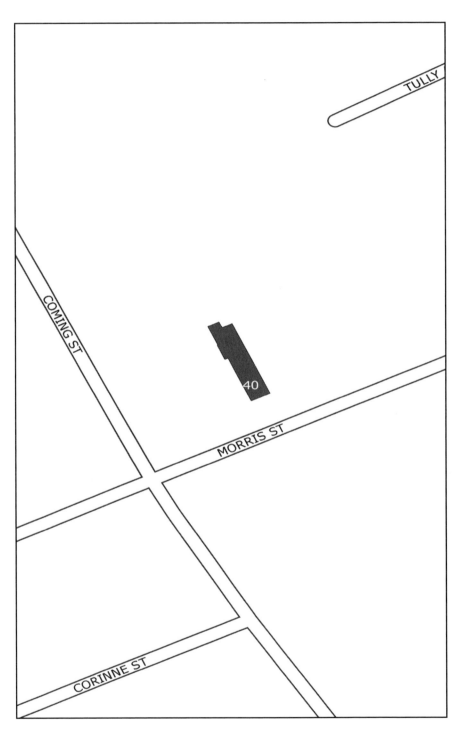

40 Morris Street.

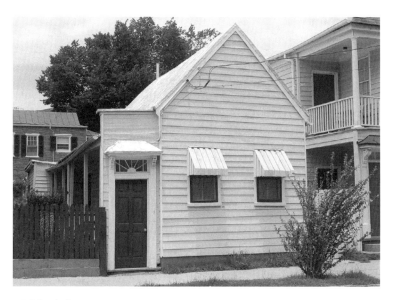

40 Morris Street.

40 MORRIS STREET

This very simple cottage on the north side of Morris Street has a somewhat confusing and complicated history, making its exact date of construction difficult to determine. Presumably because of its roof pitch, it has been referred to as a two-story structure, a one-and-one-half-story structure and a single-story dwelling interchangeably throughout its history. Records indicate that there was a structure on this lot as early as 1869. Tax records suggest that it was a two-story wooden dwelling. At that time, the property was owned by Robert Carlos De Large. He sold the property to Octavia M. and Julia De Large in 1874 for five dollars and "the love and affection I have for them," but the tax records continue to list him as the owner. The references for the building change to a single-story wooden structure in the tax records, but not on historical maps in 1881, when the property was owned by George H. Dantzman. The basic footprint of the building does not change on the early *Sanborn Fire Insurance Maps of the City of Charleston* (1884, 1888, 1893, 1901, 1929) or the *Lamblé Block Plats* of 1882, only the reference to the number of stories. Given that and the simplicity of the structure, it would seem more likely that it was constructed circa 1869.

Information on Julia and Octavia M. De Large was difficult to find. It would appear that they were, respectively, the mother and sister of Robert Carlos De Large. De Large was a fairly influential figure in Reconstruction in Charleston and the nation, and was considered to be one of Charleston's most prominent African American political leaders. He was born in Aiken, South Carolina, on March 15, 1842. He graduated from high school there and then worked as a farmer as a very young adult. Prior to the Civil War, he was a tailor in Charleston. At the age of twenty-six, he was a delegate to the South Carolina Constitutional Convention (1868), and then a member of the South Carolina House of Representatives from 1868 until 1870. In 1870, De Large was elected land commissioner for the state, in which capacity he served until his election to the United States House of Representatives that same year.

De Large served in the United States House of Representatives from March 4, 1871, until January 24, 1873, when the seat was declared vacant two months early as the result of an election challenge initiated by Sheriff Christopher C. Bowen. After leaving the United States House of Representatives, he served as a local magistrate until his death in Charleston on February 14, 1874. No record can be found regarding how or where he died, but his obituary mentioned that he had suffered a long illness and been bedridden for three weeks prior to his death.

Determining his family composition is difficult. One secondary source states that he was married to G.M. De Large and had at least twelve children. The 1870 census lists R.C. De Large (state land commissioner, twenty-eight years old), G.M. De Large (twenty-five years old) and Victoria De Large (three years old) living in Columbia. At the same time, Robert C. De Large, Mary De Large and Victoria De Large, all of comparable ages, can be found in Charleston living with Julia and O.M. De Large. One of the deeds regarding the sale of 40 Morris Street lists May or Mary Georgianna as his wife, so perhaps De Large and his family were actually counted in the census twice.

George H. Dantzman purchased the property in July 1881 from Octavia and Julia De Large. Dantzman was born in South Carolina of a German father and African American mother in April 1840. He worked in various jobs in Charleston, such as a messenger and a postal clerk. His wife, Lena, was almost twenty years his junior. The exact date of their marriage is unknown, but they did have a daughter, Sarah or Sallie, born in 1874. Sallie inherited the property after her father died in July 1904 from cerebral hemorrhage and held it until 1917. During that time, she lived at 155 Coming Street and was employed as a teacher.

No one from the De Large or Dantzman families ever occupied the house at 40 Morris Street. The cottage was never owner-occupied until it was purchased in 1949 by an African American couple, Walter and Mae

Sanford. Walter Sanford was a barber and his wife was a nurse. They owned and occupied the house until they sold it to the current owner in 1981, who also uses the property for investment purposes.

Generally speaking, this house was occupied by African American residents through at least 1961. Until the property was purchased by the Sanfords, the tenants only stayed for a year or two. The occupants were employed in a wide variety of jobs such as a "drummer" (likely a salesman rather than a musician), a cook, laundresses, a waiter, a drayman, a cabinet maker and a carpenter. The earliest known tenants were the Jones family, who were discussed in detail in the section about 277 Coming Street. They occupied the house for at least the years 1869 and 1870. The only tenants that stayed in the house for any length of time were Richard G. Pinckney and his wife Anna (Steinmitz). The Pinckneys lived in the house from 1896 through 1907. Pinckney, born in South Carolina in 1856, was employed as a driver by various companies in the city. They were married in Charleston in April 1884. There is no record of them having had any children, but neither of them can be found in any census. Richard Pinckney died in Charleston in 1917. No records can be found indicating the fate of his wife.

The physical fabric of this cottage has not changed considerably over time. A small addition was constructed at the rear prior to 1888. Records following the earthquake of 1886 indicate that the foundation and chimneys needed to be rebuilt. Whether that was done or not is unknown and the chimneys have since been removed. At some point between 1944 and 1951, the rear was enlarged again, encompassing the older addition and more than doubling the size of the original house.

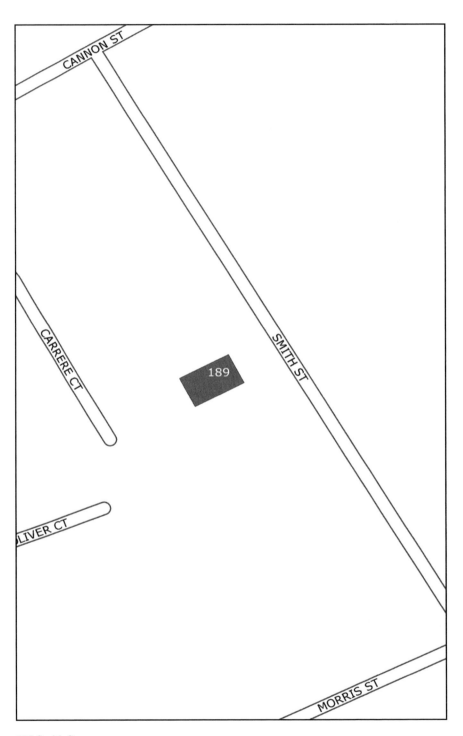

189 Smith Street.

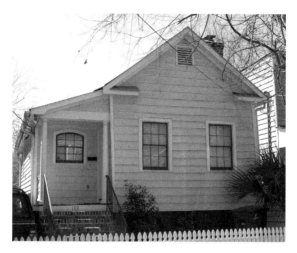

189 Smith Street.

189 SMITH STREET (FORMERLY 91 SMITH STREET)

This antebellum cottage located on the west side of Smith Street was constructed before 1853 and likely commissioned by Robert W. Disher. It is difficult to discern when he actually acquired the lot, but when he sold it in 1853, it was with "buildings thereon." Disher was a wealthy butcher and farmer, born in 1811 in South Carolina. Details of his early life are unknown. By 1850, he was married and had the first four of eight children: William (b. 1833), Catharine (b. 1836), Sarah Ann (b. 1846) and Robert (b. 1848). By 1860, Mary (b. 1849), Steadman (b. 1850), Florence (b. 1856) and Elizabeth (b. 1860) had been born and several of the oldest children had left the house. Disher held a large number of slaves before the Civil War and employed three to four domestic servants after the war. He died in 1878, at the age of sixty-seven, leaving a rather large estate to his wife, Martha.

Robert Disher sold the property in 1853, without ever having resided there, to a "free person of color," Harriett Beaufort Trescot (sometimes Trescott), who was referred to as "mulatto" in most records. It does not appear that Ms. Trescot ever lived in the house at 189 Smith Street, either. She also owned property in Goose Creek, and on Norman and Spring Streets in Charleston. According to various records, Mrs. Trescot lived in several different places on the peninsula in the 1850s and '60s. Presumably married, she resided with Paul Trescot on Spring Street and Norman Street for brief periods during these decades, and again in 1870. Paul was a "mulatto" butcher born in South Carolina in 1810. They had a large family of eight or nine children. In 1860, the children were William (b. 1844), John (b. 1844), Sarah (b. 1846), Paul (b. 1848), Joseph (b. 1853), Hariot (b. 1855), Celia (b. 1857) and James (b. 1859). The 1870 census indicates that they had another son, Dave (b. 1851), but he does not appear in any other census before or after this one. During the times that she resided without Paul Trescot, she worked as a dressmaker. Paul Trescot Sr. died in 1875, and Harriett went to live with her son, Paul, and his wife, Ocalla, on Ashley Avenue. The date of her death is unknown.

None of the members of the family prior to the births of Hariot and Celia could read or write, but those two were able to go to school. Nevertheless, it appears that the men in the family were fairly successful in their lives. William, James and Paul Jr. followed in their father's footsteps and were all butchers. Paul and James had their own butcher shop, P & J Trescot, at the Market, which slowly expanded over the years from one stall to three. William also worked as a butcher at the Market, but separate from his brothers. By the end of the nineteenth century, most of the family was living in either 101 Ashley Avenue or 210 Spring Street.

By 1861, the tax records indicate that a Henry Trescot owned the parcel, but there is no deed that shows a transfer of ownership between a Henry Trescot and Harriett. Quite possibly "Henry" is a typographical error. Frequently when a parcel was purchased in a woman's name, or transferred to her name, the husband's, father's or son's name appears on the tax records and in the city directories rather than the woman's name. Alternately, perhaps the assessor of the time assumed that "Harriett" was actually an error.

Number 189 Smith Street was occupied by African American residents exclusively from 1890 through 1961. All of these residents were renters, employed in such occupations as a waiter, laborers, laundresses, carpenters and a cook. Very few of them stayed in the house more than two or three years.

The first known occupant and tenant in 1861 was Miss Eliza Ogier. Not much more can be found beyond her name and the fact that she was white. To further add to the lack of information, it is difficult, if not impossible, to know who resided in the house between 1861 and 1890 (with the exception of the Jones family in 1869 and '79), other than the fact that it was never owner-occupied during those years.

In 1890, Joseph M. Parker moved into the cottage. He was an African American waiter and it does not appear that he was married during his residence in the cottage. He resided there through 1895. No other information can be found about Mr. Parker or his life.

An Architectural Tradition

Through the first half of the twentieth century, the occupants are difficult to trace. They worked in unskilled occupations such as laundresses, cooks, a driver and a laborer. The names of the occupants are similar in ways that make one think it is possible there were many errors made in the city directories regarding the occupancy of this house. For instance, Julia Getty is listed there in 1918, then Diana Getty in 1919. From 1920 through 1922, Diana Gethers occupied the house, followed by Louis Gethers on and off through 1930. None of these people can be found in any other historical documents referenced for this work.

Around 1942, Julius Warley (or Weiley) and his wife Lottie (or Lawdy), an African American couple, moved into the house. Julius and Lottie were married in 1921, at the ages of twenty-three and fourteen, respectively. They had one adopted son, Ernest (b. 1927), when they moved into the house, and there is no evidence suggesting any other children. The couple was born in South Carolina. Julius was one of five children born to Julius and Julia Warley. He was born in 1898 and grew up on Ashley Avenue in Charleston. He worked as a carpenter until he died in 1965. The family resided in the house through at least 1960.

This house has undergone little changes in footprint, but its original character has been greatly altered. In 1887, the house had a cedar shingle roof, which was replaced by a standing-seam metal roof, which was not an uncommon occurrence in Charleston, and was related to fire safety. Most of the piazza was enclosed by 1986. In 1994, the original simple piazza screen was removed and replaced with the present-day configuration.

PART III

THE EAST SIDE

East of Rutledge Avenue and South of Line Street

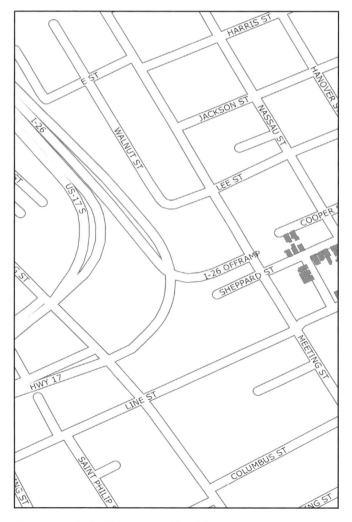

Cottages studied within the east side of the peninsula.

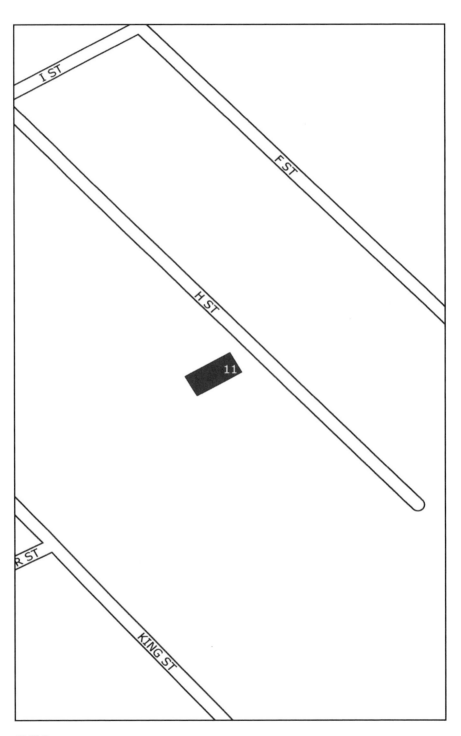

11 H Street.

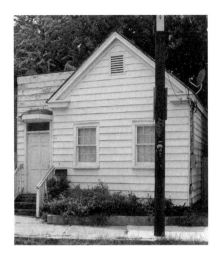

11 H Street.

11 H Street

Number 11 H Street is a rectangular cottage located on the west side of the street behind, but not associated with, 688 King Street. H Street was part of the subdivision of the Blake Lands in 1882. Adeline Buggel purchased two lots on H Street during the summer of 1882, and commissioned the construction of four single-story wooden houses on the lots by 1883. Adeline Buggel was the widow of John F. Buggel, a fairly prosperous grocer in Charleston. The Buggels were both born in Germany, John in 1838 and Adeline in 1833. They were married around 1860, and were living in Charleston by that time. The location of the Buggels' store is unknown, but it was most likely on upper King Street near or in their residence of 690 King Street. John Buggel died in 1873, leaving Adeline with four young children to raise. She never remarried, but was able to care for her family by investing money in property throughout the city, and she kept the store her husband willed to her. By the time she died (of pneumonia) in 1912, Adeline Buggel owned approximately seven investment properties, several of which were on H Street.

After Mrs. Buggel died, 11 H Street changed hands a few times before it was purchased by Rosa (Singleton) Cuttino in 1915. Her life is somewhat difficult to piece together. Ms. Cuttino was a formerly enslaved African American, born in 1855 to Benjamin and Hagar Singleton and was one of six children. She was illiterate and worked as a laundress for private families. By 1910, she is listed as a widow in the census records, living alone in a different house on H Street, possibly in one of Adeline Buggel's investment properties. The name of her husband and the date of their marriage are unknown. It does not appear that she ever had any children. Ms. Cuttino occupied the house along with her brother, Harry Singleton, until her death in 1921, and then the property was passed down to her brothers.

The house was occupied by renters until the brothers sold it to Edward Washington in 1929. He and his wife, Ella, moved into the house immediately. Since Edward Washington is such a common name, definitive records regarding his life are difficult to find. One Edward Washington married Ella Robinson in 1924. Before moving to H Street, it seems that they resided in the Rosemont neighborhood, where Edward was employed by Riverside Ironworks. Washington died in 1929, shortly after moving into his new home. The cause of his death cannot be found. He left the property to his wife. Mrs. Washington occupied the house on and off through 1968, but held it until her death in 1978, after which time it was inherited by her grandchildren. During that time she was employed in various capacities such as a laundress, a cook or a maid. Throughout its history, 11 H Street was primarily used as investment property and was generally occupied by low-income African Americans, which is typical of the entirety of H Street and the surrounding neighborhood.

This cottage experienced at least two fires in the late twentieth century and stood vacant for over a decade. In 2001, the cottage was purchased by Charleston Habitat for Humanity, Inc., and renovated.

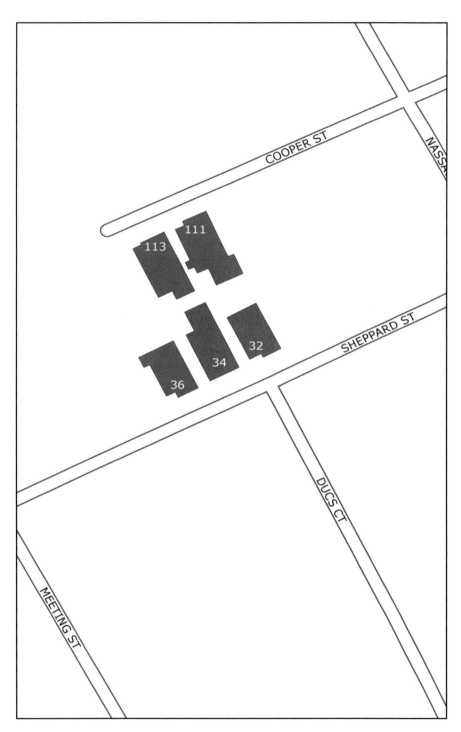

111 and 113 Cooper Street, and 32, 34 and 36 Sheppard Street.

111 AND 113 COOPER STREET, AND 32, 34 AND 36 SHEPPARD STREET

All five of these buildings (along with 115 Cooper Street, which is now gone) were constructed at the same time by the same owner and carpenter. They are all similar in detail and were constructed in identical form. They were constructed on a large parcel of land previously owned by the Enterprise Railroad Company that ran between Cooper and Sheppard Streets to the north and south, and Nassau and Meeting Streets to the east and west. After they were constructed, the events that took place inside their walls all seem to be intermingled and form a cohesive, tight-knit community. Tenants and owners change often, but are frequently part of the same families. Many of these families had lived in the neighborhood for a generation, at least.

On February 27, 1899, William B. Cohen and Levi (Lee) Loeb purchased the property for $4,300 and subdivided it into six building lots. By July 17, 1899, less than five months later, the cottages at 32, 34 and 36 Sheppard Street were constructed and the properties were sold to Ada and Ishum Lanier. By April 18, 1900, the houses at 111, 113 and 115 Cooper Street were constructed and also sold to Ada and Ishum Lanier. The Sheppard Street properties were sold for $2,600 and the Cooper Street properties sold for $2,100. An explanation for this lack of a profit is simple. At the turn of the twentieth century, the city was experiencing a severe economic slump. One contributing factor was the hurricane of 1893. It struck the city with 120-mile-per-hour winds, doing $1.16 million worth of property damage. It all but destroyed the phosphate mining and rice industries that had sustained the city in previous decades, but were beginning to decline before the hurricane struck. By the end of the decade, trade through Charleston's port was about 30 percent of what it had been in 1890, and the value of Charleston's real estate tanked as well. It declined from $25 million in 1895 to $19 million in 1904. Loeb was heavily invested in real estate in Charleston. Between 1888 and 1897, Loeb obtained mortgages on twenty-two different parcels within the city of Charleston.

In addition to Loeb's real estate investments, he and William Cohen (who was his brother-in-law) worked for William's father, Louis Cohen. Louis Cohen ran a dry goods store or department store (Louis Cohen & Company) at 232–234 King Street. Not only did they all work together, but the entire family lived under one roof as well. Often there were as many as nine family members and three or four servants living in the house at 128 Wentworth Street. After Louis Cohen retired, most if not all of the family moved to 53 Gibbes Street.

Lee Loeb was born of German parents in South Carolina in 1846. He married Louis Cohen's daughter, Bluhma, in 1878. Blumha was born in South Carolina in 1858. Her parents, Louis and Cecelia Cohen, were also from Germany, immigrating to the United States in 1850. Lee and Bluhma never had any children. In 1905, perhaps relating to financial hardship, Lee Loeb committed suicide by shooting himself.

William Cohen was born in 1860. He married Sarah in 1887, and they had three children. Only two of the children were living by 1900—their son, Sidney (b. 1890), and their daughter, Hellen (b. 1894). Sarah Cohen died in the Gibbes Street house in 1928 of "cerebral softening" at the age of sixty-four years old, so perhaps she had dementia or died form a stroke. William Cohen died a few years later, in July 1934, from colon cancer.

The story of Sidney Cohen's life is an interesting one. Cohen was educated at the University of South Carolina (USC) and the University of Pennsylvania, after which he returned to Charleston to be a reporter for the *News and Courier*. He also taught at USC and published a book on antebellum magazines of Charleston. In 1915, he was reporting on the Democratic primary for the mayoral election between John P. Grace and Tristram T. Hyde. The whole event turned so violent that the governor had to send in the militia to keep order. During a recount of the ballots, a ballot box was tossed out the window, gunfire broke out and Sidney Cohen was killed by a stray bullet. He died at the age of twenty-four.

As previously stated, all six parcels were purchased by Ada and Ishum Frank Lanier in 1899 and 1900, and it would appear that Ishum Lanier constructed all of the houses. Although there are no records specifically stating that he built the houses, he was a building contractor living at 20

Sheppard Street with his brother, an electrician, at the time of construction. Lanier was involved in construction projects all over the region. Documents have him working as far from the city as Millbrook plantation.

Lanier and his wife moved into 34 Sheppard Street after construction. Ishum Lanier married Ada Gray Leggett in Charleston in July 1895. The Laniers were both born in North Carolina, Ishum in 1851 and Ada in 1872. It is likely that Ada and Ishum met in Charleston, as Ada's family (the Leggetts) also lived on Sheppard Street in 1890s. It seems that Ada was Lanier's second wife, as his estate papers indicate additional children not related to Ada. No record in any census can be found of this previous family. Ishum and Ada had a short and sorrowful marriage.

When the Laniers moved into 34 Sheppard Street at the end of 1899, they lost their fourteen-month-old son, Linen, from "marasmus and asthenia" (protein-energy malnutrition and generalized weakness). In 1900, Ada gave birth to a daughter, Tena. Just two years later, Ada gave birth to their second daughter, Ina. Sadly, Ada died in the house from "Grippe" (influenza) and pneumonia on April 13, 1902, only three weeks after Ina's birth. Ada was only thirty years old.

One can only imagine the difficulty of a single man raising two small daughters without the aid of a wife or mother figure. Less than one year later, Ishum was remarried, this time to Lula Rachel Sharp, who was born in 1881. Lanier and his new wife remained at 34 Sheppard Street for only one more year before moving to a house on Nassau Street just a block away. Lula and Ishum had four children together, but only one (a son, James Clay) survived into adulthood. He was born in 1911. The other three children died early in life—two as newborns and one at the age of three.

In 1916, Tena married a barber, Sylvester Douglas, and the couple moved into another cottage on Nassau Street. The rest of the family remained at 115 (or 117—the records are unclear) Nassau Street until Lanier died from "chronic nephritis" (kidney infections) at the age of sixty-eight in 1919. Immediately following his death, Lula, Ina and James moved to Dorchester County to live near Lula's brother and family. In August 1920, only one day apart from each other, Lula and Ina got remarried and married respectively. Lula married David G. Myers, and Ina married Frank W. Broome.

There was a fair amount of strife between the family members and the executor of Lanier's estate, James Blank. It took almost ten years and several lawsuits to settle Lanier's estate. These six properties were inherited by Tena Lanier Douglas after her mother's death, but not transferred into her name until 1916. Other landholdings were split in various ways between Ina, James and Lula. By the time of Ishum Lanier's death, he had amassed a

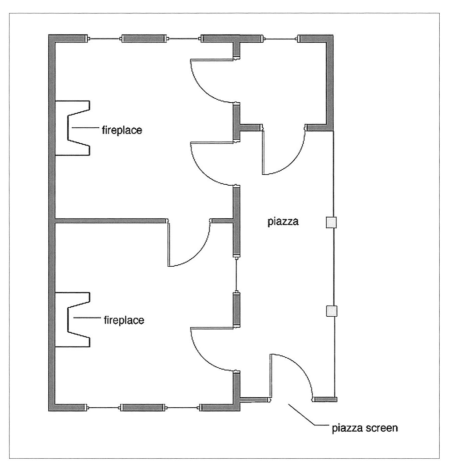

Typical floor plan of a cottage constructed or modified by Ishum Lanier.

small fortune in real estate. He bought and sold properties mostly on the east side, but also in the lower peninsula.

The physical form of these houses varied slightly in plan from the traditional two-room cottage. When these houses were constructed, the rear portion of what would have been open piazza was claimed as interior space. What this area was used for is unknown. Other than that alteration, the buildings were constructed in the same form as older cottages, with a traditional piazza and piazza screen, a gable roof and a central chimney. Over time some details in the piazza screens have been lost, and piazzas have been partially or fully enclosed. Despite these, and other more subtle, alterations, the cottages on Sheppard and Cooper Streets continue to speak of an earlier era in Charleston.

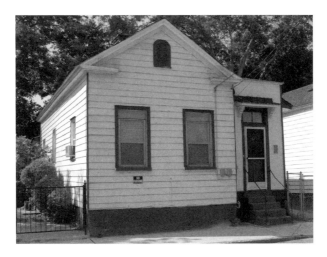

111 Cooper Street.

111 Cooper Street

111 Cooper Street (69 Cooper Street before 1958) was occupied by a variety of individuals and families through 1961. During that time it was never owner-occupied and the majority of the residents were white, low- to middle-class workers, similar to the general makeup of the neighborhood over time. The house was not occupied by African Americans until 1955. A large number of the residents were employed by Southern Railway. Others were carpenters, factory workers or employed by the United States Post Office and the navy yard. As many as eight people lived in the house at once, but only one family lived there for more than two or three years. The first residents of the cottage were James and Mary Saxton. Saxton was a millworker, and they only lived in the house for one year. No other information can be found about this couple.

The family that lived in the house the longest was the Anderson family. George E. Anderson and his wife, Josephine, moved into the house in 1916, and lived there through 1923 with their two sons, Archie and Eugene, and Anderson's brother, James. Anderson worked as a carpenter, and Archie and James were employed as brakemen for Southern Railway. The entire family was born in South Carolina. George was born in 1871, Josephine in 1875, Archie in 1900, Eugene in 1905 and James in 1887. What happened to this family after they left Cooper Street is unknown.

In 1927, William B. Murray and his wife, Lillie, moved into the house. Little can be found regarding this couple. William was employed by Southern

Railway, and he died in the house in 1930, but records of the cause of his death cannot be found. Lillie stayed for one more year before disappearing from the records entirely. In 1938, Charles and Alma Anderson began renting the cottage. They were a family of six, but no specifics can be found regarding the makeup of their family. Charles worked as a rigger on the naval base. He died while living on Cooper Street in 1940. After he died, his wife and family remained in the house and Alma took employment at the General Asbestos and Rubber Company, then as a city bus driver. She remained in the house through at least 1945. Again, no other information can be found.

After 1945, the residents were a series of short-term renters, white and African American. They were employed by the United States Post Office, the United States Coast Guard, Blanch Darby Florist and a cab company.

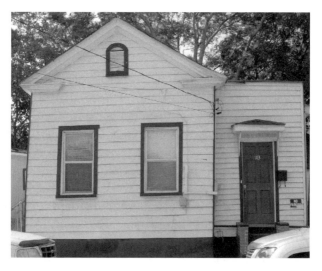

113 Cooper Street.

113 Cooper Street

Number 113 Cooper Street (71 Cooper Street before 1958) was also occupied by a wide variety of individuals and families through 1961. Similar to 111 Cooper, it was never owner-occupied, and only one African American occupied the house during this time and only for one year. The first residents of the house in 1900 were Pinckney D. and Minnie S. Cummings, born in South Carolina in 1865 and 1871, respectively. Mr. Cummings was employed as an electrician and mechanic for the street railway in Charleston. The Cummings family moved into the house with two small children, both sons, Le Roy (b. 1893) and Kin (b. 1898), and one more on the way. Ultimately, they had four children, three sons and a daughter. Their third son was Arthur B. (b. 1901), and their daughter was Helen M. (b. 1909). Cummings died in 1932. Documents for the cause of his death cannot be found.

For the next decade and a half, the building was occupied by small families and individuals who only stayed for a year or two. They worked in local factories mostly, or for the Consolidated Railway Company. From 1917 through 1921, the house was occupied by Wingate and Rosalie Muckenfuss and their two daughters, Clara (b. 1907) and Maude (b. 1915). Muckenfuss was born in Yamasee, South Carolina, into a family of nine. He married Rosalie Cloea Roumillet in 1906. Rosalie was also born into a large family in 1879, and raised on Nassau Street. Her family saw its share of heartache when only three of her nine siblings survived into adulthood. Muckenfuss held various positions for the Consolidated Railway Company, including general inspector and air brake inspector. After they left Cooper Street, they moved into an apartment on Ann Street for a few years, and then purchased a house in the Rose Garden neighborhood in the upper peninsula. Wingate died in 1943, and Rosalie four years later.

After the Muckenfuss family moved from the house, it was occupied by a variety of blue-collar families who only stayed for a year or two, with one exception. In 1936, Mrs. Hattie Campbell, a widow (of John N. Campbell), and her daughter moved into the house with John A. Smith and his wife, Maggie. They all lived together through at least 1945, and Mrs. Campbell stayed through 1948. Other members of the Campbell family moved in and out of the house over time. In 1940, there were five adults and an unknown number of children living in this tiny house! In the 1950s and early 1960s, the house again was home to a variety of individuals and families. They were typically blue-collar workers employed in such jobs as a welder, a printer, a city employee in the Public Works Department and a helper on the navy base. The first African American to occupy this house was in 1955. He was Herbert R. Miller, who was employed as a printer. He lived in the house alone and was only recorded as residing there in 1955.

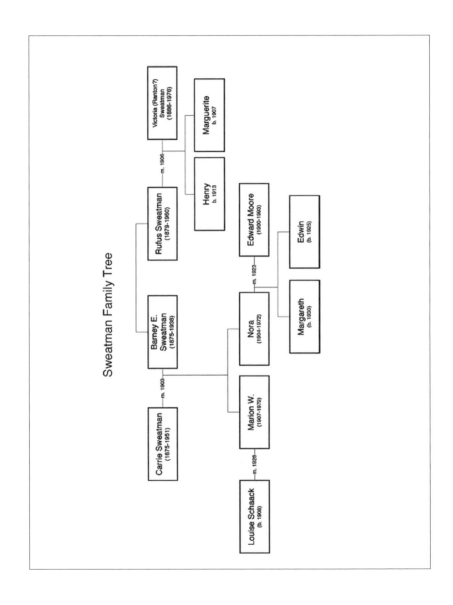

Sweatman Family Tree

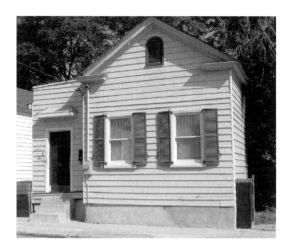

32 Sheppard Street.

32 Sheppard Street

Number 32 Sheppard Street was home to a variety of white renters throughout its history. The first tenants, who only lived in the house for one year, were Edward and Ida (Albers) Friend. Edward was born in South Carolina in 1876 and Ida was born in New York in 1877. The couple married in Charleston in May 1899 and adopted a thirteen-year-old daughter, Lillie, by 1900. Friend worked for the Consolidated Railway Company as a conductor. The small family did not stay in Charleston long before relocating to Norfolk, Virginia. After the Friends moved out, the house was occupied by a series of short-term white tenants. They were employed in such positions as a life insurance agent, a farmer, a grocer, a switchman for the Southern Railway and a clerk, to name a few.

In 1921, Carrie Sweatman purchased the property and continued to use it for investment purposes. In 1932, she sold it to her son, Marion, for five dollars. Marion and his wife, Louise (Schaack), married for fours years by this point, moved in shortly after the purchase and remained there through 1945. Marion Sweatman was born in 1907, and grew up on Cooper Street in Charleston. His father, Barney E. Sweatman, was a carpenter, born in Summerville, South Carolina. Louise was born in Charleston in 1908 to Edward F. and Henrietta Schaack of Germany. Her father was a railroad conductor. Marion worked in various jobs while living on Sheppard Street. He worked for the City of Charleston, and as a paperhanger and a painter. Louise worked as a telephone operator for a time. Whether or not they had any children is unknown. Marion died in 1979.

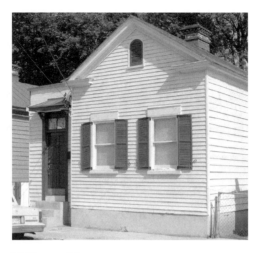

34 Sheppard Street.

34 Sheppard Street

As previously stated, the earliest residents of this cottage were Ishum and Ada Lanier, who moved in immediately after construction. Ishum remained in the house through Ada's death and for the first couple years of marriage to Lula. In 1905, Ishum and Lula began to rent out the house after they relocated to another house on Nassau Street. The earliest tenants only stayed for a year or two and worked in a variety of professions such as a policeman, a paperhanger, a painter and an insurance agent.

In 1912, Barney Sweatman's older brother and family began to rent the house. Rufus Westley and Victoria Adeline (Ranton) Sweatman lived in the house with their young children until 1919, when they moved to 43 Sheppard Street. Their older child, Marguerite, was born in 1907, and Henry was born in the house in 1912. Rufus, born in 1877, worked as a paperhanger and painter throughout his life. When finances were tight in the 1920s, the Sweatmans took in a family of renters to help make ends meet. The Sweatmans remained in the neighborhood though at least the 1930s. Rufus died in 1960, and Victoria in 1976, at the age of ninety.

In 1920, after the death of her father, Tena Lanier Douglas moved into the house with her husband of four years, Sylvester. Sylvester was employed in myriad occupations throughout the city, such as a steel worker, a machinist, a chauffeur for the Charleston Police Department and a barber! While living at this house, they had two sons, Harry (b. 1917) and Carl (b. 1918). In 1920, they also had Sylvester's sisters-in-law, Lilien and Rubie Donnelly, residing with them in that tiny house. Ultimately they would have seven children and end up on Columbus Street as none of the real estate Tena inherited would accommodate such an enormous family.

In 1921, the Douglas family moved out of the house and sold the property. It sold again in 1925, and was purchased by Nora (Sweatman) Moore. She and her husband, Edward, owned and lived in the house through 1955, where they raised two children, Margareth (b. 1930) and Edwin (b. 1925). Married in 1923, Edward and Nora likely met in the neighborhood as they were both raised on Cooper Street. Nora was the daughter of Barney Sweatman, brother of Marion, and was born in 1904. Edward was born in 1900 to Mr. and Mrs. Alex Moore. Edward's father emigrated from Ireland and worked as a superintendent at the oil refinery. Edward was one of eight children.

Following in his father's footsteps, Edward worked at Standard Oil Company of New Jersey in several capacities through 1951. In his later years, he was employed as a gardener. Edward lived to be ninety-three years old, but lost his wife in 1972—twenty-one years earlier.

The Moores sold the property to the first African American owner and occupant, Louise R. Clay, who moved into the house with seven children! Not much else can be found about this family. They resided there until 1971.

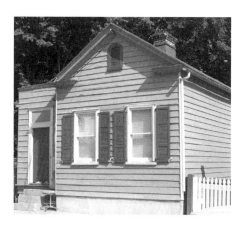

36 Sheppard Street.

36 Sheppard Street

Number 36 Sheppard Street, like its sister houses, was occupied predominantly by a variety of white tenants, and was rarely ever owner-occupied. The first tenants in the house in 1900 were George H. Fogle, his wife Lucia, his brother, William, and his sister-in-law, Mattie. George was employed as a carpenter and his brother was a police officer. They resided in house for only three years.

Various short-term tenants occupied the cottage for the next five years until the Garrys took up residence in 1908. Archie J. Garry and his wife Martha raised their only son, Archie Jr. (b. 1904), in the house. Archie Garry Sr. and his wife were both born in South Carolina, Archie in 1868 and Martha fourteen years later. Garry was employed as a foreman in several factories throughout the city. In 1925, Martha predeceased her husband and the cause of her death cannot be found. After 1932, the two men moved out of Charleston. There is no evidence that either one of the men ever remarried or married. Archie Jr. died in Charleston County in 1946. The date and location of his father's death is unknown.

Barney and Carrie Sweatman purchased the property in 1935 and moved in. Barney died in 1938 while living in the house. Records indicate that Carrie may have remained in the house after his death, but took in boarders to help make ends meet. Carrie was living at the house when she died in 1951, at the age of seventy-six. After her death, ownership of the parcel passed to her children, Marion Sweatman and Nora Sweatman Moore, who retained it for about eight years as investment property. The parcel was purchased by the current owners in 1963 and continues to be a rental unit.

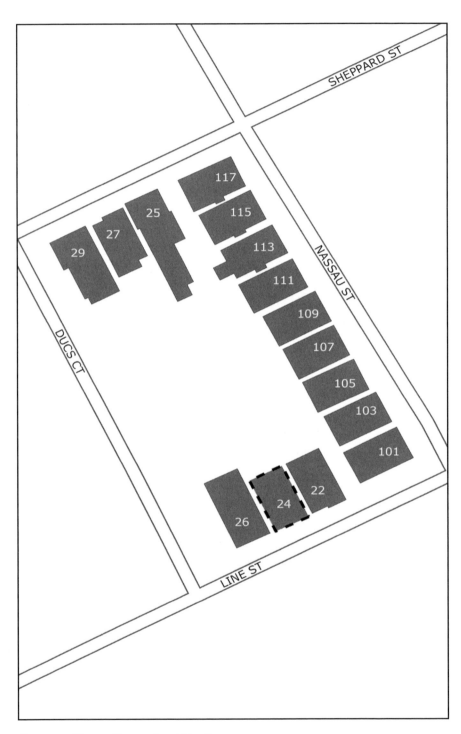

Cottages at Nassau, Sheppard and Line Streets.

Nassau, Sheppard and Line Street Complex

This complex of fourteen (originally fifteen) cottages is located primarily on the east side of Nassau Street with two (formerly three) adjacent cottages on the north side of Line Street and three on the south side of Sheppard Street. They are different from any of the other buildings researched for this book. They have the same form as the typical freedman's cottage, but were constructed completely out of concrete, interior walls and all. At first glance, they may appear to be cottages either built or modified in the 1950s, but in fact were constructed much earlier.

Between 1908 and 1911, Henry A. Duc Jr. sold a large and mostly undeveloped parcel in pieces (bounded by Nassau Street on the east, Line Street on the south, Sheppard Street on the north and parcels on the west side of Duc's Court on the west), to Ishum Lanier. It is unclear exactly when each building was constructed, but by 1910 all of the cottages were built and occupied. All of the structures were commissioned, and likely constructed, by Lanier as well. Similar to the cottages he constructed on Sheppard and Cooper Streets about a decade earlier, these buildings were originally built with the rear of what would have been the piazza being interior space.

Given that concrete was not widely used in the United States until the 1920s, it would seem these cottages were technologically advanced for their time. However, there were at least two concrete companies in Charleston at this time and other concrete projects were underway right around the time of their construction, such as the Charleston sea walls in 1909 to 1911, then

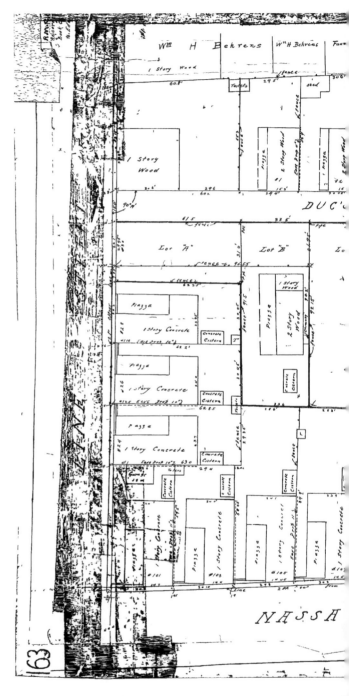

1920 plat of the lands belonging to the estate of Ishiam Lanier. Plat Book C, page 163. On file with the Charleston County RMC Office.

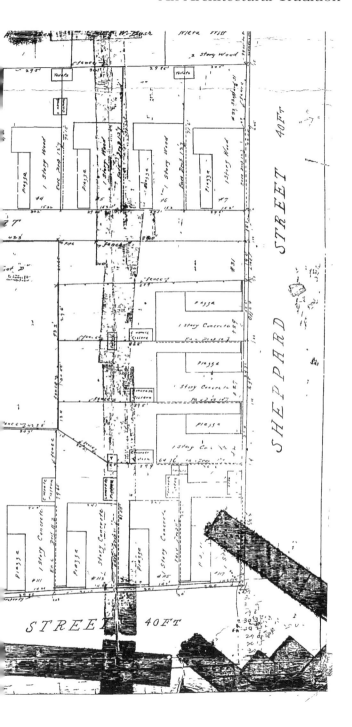

1917 to 1919. J.C. Long is often given credit for his innovative construction techniques when he designed the hurricane-resistant house on Mount Pleasant Street out of concrete in the 1930s. All of these cottages and the sea walls predate J.C. Long's project by at least one generation.

A very detailed plat of the complex from 1920 provides an excellent idea of what life was like in these particular cottages. Each house was equipped with a rectangular concrete cistern directly behind the house on the property line. In most instances, there was also an outhouse or privy for each cottage. It consisted of one building, presumably housing two toilets, that was shared by two houses as it straddled the property line. These lots were typically about thirty feet wide by sixty-two to eighty-five feet deep, making the proximity of the "toilets" and the cisterns unhealthy to say the least. The timing of their construction barely predates laws in the city prohibiting privies and outhouses. By ordinance ratified in 1909, all privies were to be destroyed and privy vaults filled by January 1, 1910. The same fate was ordered for privies and privy vaults on any street north of Broad within six months of the sewer being constructed. The sewer was not constructed in this area until 1923, despite a recognized need for better sanitation throughout the 1910s. In 1922, in his annual report to the mayor, the city engineer cited World War I as a cause for halting the progress on sewer construction started before the war. He stated that there was a lack of available materials for construction during the war.

For the most part, throughout the first half of the twentieth century, very few of the houses were owner-occupied. With few exceptions the cottages were occupied by low- to middle-income white families and individuals. With some exceptions, few occupants resided in this neighborhood for more than a few years. A large number of the occupants were widows (possibly from World War II) and men and women employed by the Works Progress Administration (WPA).

The WPA was an enormous undertaking by the United States Federal government to help stimulate the economy and provide jobs during the Great Depression (1929–39). The WPA was created in 1935 by an order of Franklin Delano Roosevelt and activated by congressional funding that same year. It continued relief programs started in 1932 under Herbert Hoover. Under this program, many public projects, buildings and roads were completed. It also operated large literacy and arts projects, and distributed food and clothing to the needy. Many of the women employed by the WPA were taught to operate sewing machines so they could make clothing, supplies and bedding for local orphanages and hospitals.

Until the program was discontinued in 1943, the various programs of the WPA added up to the largest employment base in the country. The program ended with the onset of World War II as war production eliminated unemployment, making this program unnecessary. To give you an idea of the enormity of this program, the WPA employed approximately 3.3 million people in November 1938. Approximately $11.4 billion was spent on WPA projects through June 1941. Most of that money was spent on highway, road and street projects, but $1 billion of it was spent on welfare projects, including sewing projects for women, the distribution of surplus commodities and school lunch projects. Many of the women living in this neighborhood in the late 1930s and early '40s were employed in this capacity. It is important to keep in mind that this program was not a great panacea. Workers were not allowed to work more that thirty hours per week and only one person per family was eligible to work within this program. Wages were supposed to be equal to prevailing wages in the area and were based on skill level. Pay ranged from nineteen to ninety-four dollars per month. Average rent for this block of houses in 1930 was eighteen dollars per month. Just within this small neighborhood were many women, and a few men, having to support families of four or more on these wages.

After Lanier died in 1919, some of the parcels were inherited by his wife, Lula, and some were sold off individually by his estate in 1920. Several of the parcels were sold to the same individuals or families, and remained in their possession until the 1960s. Lula inherited 109 through 117 Nassau Street, and with the exception of 105 Nassau Street, all the rest of the parcels were either purchased by Harris Livingstain or Lillye Berlinsky (the family name later changed to Berlin). At some point in the twentieth century, the Livingstains and the Berlins intermarried and a few of the parcels were co-owned by both families in the 1960s. Number 105 Nassau Street was purchased by John M. Henriksen. Lula died in 1949, still in possession of four of the cottages. She split her holdings between her two children, Ina and James.

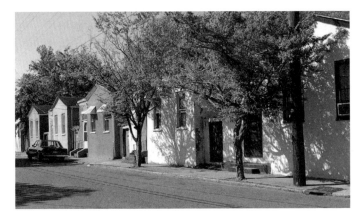

107–117 Nassau Street, a typical arrangement and detail of the fifteen cottages found at Line, Sheppard, and Nassau.

101–117 Nassau Street

For these nine buildings, still very much intact and occupied, it was more difficult to trace who exactly lived in which house and when during the twentieth century due to addressing issues. The names listed in the city directories and the census records often conflict with each other. Additionally, occupants seemed to bounce around from one house to the next from year to year. The transient nature of this particular group also made them difficult to track beyond their short stint in the neighborhood.

101 Nassau Street

The earliest known residents of this cottage were Henry H. Strickland and his wife, Ivy. They resided in the cottage in 1911, left for one year and returned again in 1913. Henry worked as a manager in some unspecified location. Beyond that, very little information can be found about this couple. Number 101 Nassau Street was left out of the 1910 census altogether, and the Stricklands disappear from the records after 1913.

An Architectural Tradition

Over the next two decades, the cottage was home to a variety of tenants. Many of them were family members of other residents in the block, or lived in other cottages in the block over time. In 1924, carpenter Lonnie Stone and his wife, Edith, occupied this cottage, and then lived at 28 Line Street in 1927. Another example is Rudolph Ham, a painter at the navy yard. He resided here in at least 1920 with his sister and niece, and Albert Ham and his family lived at 109 Nassau Street at the same time. And although their relationship is unknown, it can be safely assumed that they are related directly. After Albert and his wife left the neighborhood, Rudolph could be found living with them.

In 1926, James Andrew Manning began renting the cottage with his wife, Geanie or Janie. Little information can be found for this couple, either. They only lived in the house for about three years. Manning was a conductor for the Atlantic Coast Line Railroad.

In 1934, William Russell Weatherford and his wife, Sadie J., moved into this cottage. William was born in Augusta, Georgia, in 1895. He married Sadie Johnson in Charleston County in 1916. Sadie was born in South Carolina in 1899. By 1930, they had three children—Dorothy (b. 1918), Eastern (daughter, b. 1925) and Marvin (b. 1928). William was employed in various capacities while living in Charleston, but generally speaking, he was a carpenter. The Weatherfords occupied 101 Nassau Street through 1940, after which their residence is unknown.

Another family that occupied the cottage for more than a few years was Melvin and Ella B. Stanley. They resided here from 1950 through 1958, after which the house was vacant for more than ten years. Melvin was employed as an electrician at the navy base. It does not appear that they had any children—at least not while they lived at 101 Nassau Street. No other information can be found.

It is interesting to note that the original cistern remains standing behind the house. At some point, it was modified and is now used for storage.

103 Nassau Street

The family that resided in this block the longest in the early years was the Doars. Arthur E. Doar and his family began renting 103 Nassau Street immediately after construction in 1910. Arthur Eugene Doar married Margaret (Maggie) R. O'Brien in Charleston County in 1894. They had six children together, only five of whom were living in 1910 when they moved into the house. The children were Mary (b. 1895), Kate (b. 1898), Henry (b. 1900), Robert (b. 1903) and William (b. 1907). Arthur worked as a machinist to support his large family, and his daughter Mary started working as early as fifteen at the American Tobacco Company or "Cigar Factory" located at 701 East Bay Street. They remained in the house through 1920 and had one more child, Margaret Cecile (b. 1914). By 1930 they were living in Harleston Village, and in 1933 Arthur Doar died at the age of sixty-nine.

After the Doars relocated, the cottage was home to a variety of transient residents who remained here for only a year or two through 1938. There were single men, married couples and small families living here during that time. Their occupations included a gas maker for the power company, a blacksmith and a boiler maker.

In 1940, Harriett E. Easterby moved into the house. No employment is listed by her name in the city directories, nor is she referred to as a widow. She left the house in 1951 and no other information can be found regarding who she was.

In 1961, the cottage was owner-occupied for the first time by Genevieve Simmons Boags, who purchased it from Henry Berlin and Leo Livingstain. She held the property through 1971.

105 Nassau Street

The earliest residents of this cottage were Henry J. Massalon and his wife, Pearl. They were both born in South Carolina around 1883. Their lives were fraught with drama and sadness. They married in 1903 and had four children, two of whom died very early. In 1906, their son Thomas H. died from "defective circulation" at two days old. Then, their infant daughter, Ertha, died of pneumonia, heart failure and atelectasis (infant respiratory distress syndrome) at two days old in 1907. When they moved into this house in 1910, they had Daniel E. (b. 1908) and Jessie A. (b. 1910). Henry worked as a machinist and an electrician at the Cigar Factory. In 1912, they moved farther north on Nassau Street and then to Duc's Court by 1924. In 1925, at the age of forty-two, Henry was murdered—shot in the head. Unfortunately, this murder was not reported in the newspaper and no other information can be obtained. The fate of this rest of his family is unknown.

After the Massalons left, the cottage was occupied by a series of renters until 1922. Oddly, the tenants during this time period were all employed by the railroad or the city's street railway service. They each only stayed in the house for a year before moving on.

Number 105 Nassau Street was one of the earliest owner-occupied dwellings in the neighborhood. As previously mentioned, it was purchased by John M. Henriksen from Lanier's estate in 1920. By 1921, he and his family were living in the cottage and continued to reside there until 1947, when they sold it to the Allen family. Henriksen was born in South Carolina in 1889 into a family of seven. He married Rosa E. Janer in Charleston County in 1910 and had at least four children with her. Their children were John M. Jr. (b. 1912), Christine (sometimes Christian) (b. 1914), Robert E. (b. 1918) and James V. (b. 1923). Henriksen was employed by Momeier Electric Company as an electrician as early as 1917, and as an electrician with some unspecified company prior to that. His sons followed in his footsteps to become electricians as well, although they were employed by a different company. Robert and John Jr. resided in the house with their parents and their wives (they were married in 1936 and 1940, respectively) through 1942. John Henriksen Sr. died in 1951.

In 1946, John Henriksen sold the property to Bute Fennell, who occupied the house briefly before his death, and then willed the parcel to Claudia Allen (relationship unknown). Ms. Allen occupied the house in 1951, but then used it for investment purposes. The house remains in the possession of the Allen family.

107 Nassau Street (sometimes 105½ Nassau Street)

Another family who lived in the neighborhood immediately after construction at 107 Nassau Street was Elvis Brender and his wife, Jennie, with their children. Brender was born in Germany in 1855. He immigrated to the United States in 1873, and worked as a motorman for the street railway in the city. His wife was eighteen years his junior and born in Florida. They were married in 1893, and had four children: Mabel (b. 1895), Alvie (b. 1896), Pearl (b. 1900) and Raymond (b. 1909). They only lived in the house for one year and then disappear from the records.

After the Brenders moved out, similar to the rest of these houses, 107 was occupied by a variety of transient renters who came and went from year to year. The occupations they held varied widely. There were employees of the WPA, clerks, painters, foremen and watchmen. There was also at least one widow, and several men and women who were unemployed in the 1930s.

Edward Dennis Veno and his wife, Thelma Daisy (Bunch), began renting the house in 1948. The couple was married in Charleston County in 1931. Veno was employed as a "car body man," or a mechanic. They had two children by 1958, lived in the house through at least 1961 and were gone by 1968. It is interesting to note that a Thelma Bunch moved to 5 Duc's Court (another cottage studied for this work) in 1931, and the Veno family lived close by on Line Street and Meeting Street in the 1920s. Perhaps they met while living in this neighborhood.

109 Nassau Street (sometimes 111 Nassau Street)

The earliest known occupants of this cottage were Charles O. Brown and his family, who occupied the house in 1910 and 1911. Charles and his wife, Erika, were both born in Virginia around 1886. They were married in Virginia in 1901 and had three children by 1910. Their children were Dorothy (b. 1902), Nellie (b. 1905) and Edgar (b. 1908). Charles worked as a machinist for the railroad and they evidently moved around quite a bit as Edgar was born in North Carolina, the rest of the children were born in

Virginia and then they all moved to South Carolina. No other information can be found regarding this family.

From 1917 through 1922, Albert P. Ham and his family resided at 109 Nassau Street. They also lived at 107 Nassau Street in 1913. Albert and Ruth Estell (White) were married in Charleston County in 1911. Ruth and Albert were both born in South Carolina in 1896 and 1887, respectively. By 1920, they had had three children, but lost one. Their remaining children were Albert Jr. (b. 1915) and Wilson (b. 1917). Albert worked as a house painter. After they left Nassau Street, they went to live in Hampton Park Terrace. Albert died in 1948 and the fate of his wife is unknown.

For the next decade, the house was occupied by a series of short-term tenants. Some were widows living alone, and others were small families. The type of employment they held varies, from a stockman to an engineer.

The family that occupied this house the longest was Raymond Lamb with his wife and children, who moved in around 1934. Raymond and Venice (or Vina) were married in 1924 and moved to Charleston from Berkeley County, where Raymond had been employed by the railroad as a laborer. In Charleston he worked as a night watchman for a manufacturing company through 1940, and then was employed as a chauffeur for the Charleston Police Department. Raymond was born in South Carolina in 1904 and Venice in 1900. By 1930, they had three children, Noland (b. 1925), Vernice (b. 1927) and Mamie (b. 1929). They stayed in the house through 1945 and had three more children. The names and dates of birth of these children are unknown. While they lived in the house, Mary Burbage, widow of Thomas Burbage, also resided with them. Her relationship to them is unknown. She worked for the WPA as a "cutter" and a seamstress, and lived with them through 1942, after which she disappears from the records.

After the Lambs left the cottage, it was owner-occupied for the first time by John H. and Azalea Cass, who purchased the parcel in 1945 and moved in before 1948. They moved to this house from Aiken Street, where they had lived for about thirty years. John was a grocer born in Tennessee in 1881. He and Azalea, who was born in South Carolina in 1891, were married in 1910. Early in their marriage Azalea worked as a stenographer. They had six children together, one of whom died at birth in 1911. The other children were Mary L. (b. 1913), Winnieford (b. 1914), Gloris (b. 1915), John H. Jr. (b. 1924) and Levine (b. 1928). John died two years after moving to Nassau Street in 1950. Azalea and John Jr. remained living on Nassau Street through 1951, when Azalea sold the parcel and relocated. The parcel was sold once more before the current owners purchased it in 1978.

111 Nassau Street (sometimes 113 Nassau Street)

The earliest known resident of this cottage was Mrs. Sarah V. Poston, widow of Daniel Poston, who occupied 111 Nassau Street from 1910 through 1912. The Postons were from South Carolina and were married for forty-eight years. She had ten children, only seven of whom were living in 1910. Mrs. Poston was born in 1843 and worked as a dressmaker from her home. Two of her daughters and a boarder lived with her on Nassau Street—all three of them were employed by the Cigar Factory.

One very large family to reside in this neighborhood was the Turneys (sometimes Tierney). Joseph M. Turney and his wife, Nellie (Martin), lived in 105 or 107 Nassau Street from 1913 through 1918, and then they lived in this house from 1920 through 1922. Also residing with them was their son Vincent (b. 1920), Nellie's mother, Lilly Rourke, and Nellie's three siblings—Lottie (b. 1908), Herman (b. 1911) and Tidler (b. 1913). Turney was employed as a machinist at the navy yard, and Mrs. Rourke worked for the Cigar Factory as a cigar maker. Mrs. Rourke moved to 113 Nassau Street in 1923 and the Turneys left the city.

After the Turneys left, the cottage was occupied by a series of short-term renters, such as Sylvester and Tena Douglas, who occupied this cottage in 1926 and 1927. As previously mentioned, Tena Douglas was the daughter of the builder of these cottages, Ishum Lanier. Lanier specified in his will that she inherit no more than $100 from his estate, "as I have previously made ample advances to her." Tena had inherited the six cottages on Sheppard and Cooper Streets in 1916 after her mother died. She then sold them in 1921. Whatever happened between 1921 and 1926 that she and her husband had to live in one of her stepmother's houses is unknown. In addition, Lula Lanier did not leave anything to Tena in her will either when she died in 1949.

From 1926 through 1961, the house was occupied by a variety of tenants ranging from small families to single individuals. They were employed in such professions as carpenters, mechanics and painters, many of whom were employed by the Cigar Factory. The average length of stay was two years.

An Architectural Tradition

113 Nassau Street (sometimes 115 Nassau Street)

The earliest known residents of 113 Nassau Street were Curtis and Salina Brown, who only lived in the house for one year. Curtis worked in a dry goods store and was born in South Carolina in 1884. In 1905, he married Salina, who was born in South Carolina in 1886. By 1910, they had had three children, but only two were living: David (b. 1908) and Inez (b. 1909 or 1910). Upon leaving this house, they moved to Amherst Street in 1911.

From the earliest occupant through 1968, this cottage was occupied by a wide variety of short-term white tenants that only stayed in the house for one or two years. They were employed by the City of Charleston, the navy yard, the railroad and the Cigar Factory. There were carpenters, flagmen, bricklayers, firemen and mechanics that lived in this small house alone or with their families.

The one family that stayed in the house for more than two years lived there from 1928 through 1934. They were Benjamin M. Salisbury and his wife, Leone. They had a rather large family consisting of seven children, all of whom lived in this cottage in 1930. Benjamin and Leone were both born in South Carolina, Benjamin in 1884 and Leone in 1894. They were married in 1911. Benjamin worked as a house carpenter, and two of his children worked for a dry cleaning company. The children were Leroy (b. 1912), Vernon L. (b. 1914), Thelma M. (b. 1920), Charles (b. 1921), Helen (b. 1924), Margarette (b. 1926) and Marion (b. 1929). In 1936, this family moved to Meeting Street above the Downy Flake Doughnut Shop where Thelma worked as a clerk. Benjamin continued to work as a carpenter, and Vernon was employed as a painter.

After the Salisbury family moved to Meeting Street, the house was again home to short-term tenants who stayed there for two or three years. Interestingly enough, Vernon Salisbury returned to the house with his wife Dorothy and their child. They lived there for at least 1950–51. By then Vernon was employed as a bricklayer.

The Charleston "Freedman's Cottage"

115 Nassau Street (sometimes 117 Nassau Street)

The early records for 115 Nassau Street often conflict with those from 117 Nassau Street between the census and the city directories. Because of that, it is difficult to know with certainty who occupied these houses in the first few years after construction. It would appear that John P. Wade and his wife were the first occupants of this cottage, although the directories indicate that Ishum Lanier occupied the house early on. John P. Wade was born in South Carolina in 1852, and was employed as a mechanic at the navy yard. He married his second wife, Lizzie, in 1904. Lizzie was born in South Carolina and was twenty-five years his junior. They had three children together but had lost one by the time they moved into this house. Their children were Flora (b. 1906) and Minnie (b. 1909). John's son from his previous marriage, Charles (b. 1886), was living with them, along with a fifteen-year-old boarder as well. The family stayed in the house for one year only, and then moved from the city.

From 1918 through 1922, members of the Tanner family resided in this cottage. They were William P. Tanner, his wife, Ella C. (also Eleanor or Carrie), and James P. Tanner and his wife, Eveline (also Eunice). William and Ella were the parents of James. The whole family was born in South Carolina, William in 1856, Ella in 1857 and James and Eveline in 1887. William and Ella were married in 1877 and had six children, five of whom survived into adulthood. William held various jobs throughout his life. When William and Ella were first married, he worked as a teamster (person who drove a team of draft animals), then as a "day laborer," then a watchman for the railroad while living on Nassau Street and then in his final years he was a laborer again. William died in 1938. He outlived both his wife and James, and was forced to board with another family on Coming Street at the end of his life.

James Tanner worked as a house painter. It does not appear that he and his wife ever had any children. He died in 1922 and his widow moved to 117 Nassau Street. The fate of Eveline after 1923 is unknown.

After the Tanners left this house, it was occupied by Walter L. Edwards and his wife, Elvie. They were born in Williamsburg County, South Carolina, in 1883 and 1884, respectively. Walter was born to Henry and Jane Edwards, who were farmers and had eight children. The exact date of their marriage is unknown, but they were married and living with Walter's parents in 1900. Early in their marriage, Walter was a farm laborer on the family farm. By 1910, they had moved to Chatham, Georgia, and had the first two of their children. Walter was then employed as a conductor for the railroad and remained as such until he retired. The Edwards family returned to South Carolina, this time to Charleston, in 1918, where they had their fifth child. Their children were Ethel (b. 1905), Marie M. (b. 1908), Walter L. Jr. (b. 1911), Leona (b. 1915) and Cathelene (b. 1918). They remained at 115 Nassau Street through 1928. Walter was retired by 1926. The fate of this family after they left Nassau Street is unknown.

From 1928 through 1961, the house was occupied by a stream of transient individuals and families. They were salesmen, painters, factory workers, inspectors and carpenters. From 1936 through 1938, Mrs. Ellie Austin resided in the house. She was a widow (of V.S.) and employed by the WPA as a seamstress. At the same time, two houses away at 111 Nassau Street, were Julian Austin and his wife Mary Lee. Very little can be found regarding this couple and their relationship to Ellie Austin is unknown. Mary Lee Austin also ended up living at 115 Nassau Street in 1950–51.

117 Nassau Street

Of this group of houses, 117 Nassau Street was the most difficult one to research. For some unknown period of time around the 1920s and 1930s, there were two parcels addressed as 117 Nassau Street—this one and the parcel at the northwest corner of Nassau and Sheppard Streets. The one on that corner was a two-story, wooden, mixed-use building. It housed a grocery store on the first floor and a residence on the second. At some point, it was demolished, as the parcel is vacant now.

As previously stated, it would appear that Ishum and Lula Lanier were the first occupants of this cottage. Who lived there after this point until about 1924 is unknown. In 1924, as previously stated, the widow Eunice (Eveline) Tanner resided in the house. Strangely, another Evelyn Tanner resided here with others in 1930, but she was only eighteen years old and apparently unrelated to this Eveline Tanner. From 1925 through 1942, two widows resided in this house. The two women were not in the house at the same time all these years, but for many of them. Their names get a bit confusing when looking through the city directories, but with careful analysis between the directories and other historical documents, it seems to be manageable to some degree. The two widows are Eunice Hattie Madray and Mrs. K.L. Madray (also known as Susan). Susan was married to Keating Louis Madray (also known as K.L. Madray) and Eunice was married to Louis K. Madray. Eunice was born in South Carolina in 1894 and her husband was also born in 1894. Keating was born in 1860 and Susan's date of birth is unknown. Their husbands both died in 1924, but in separate states. Keating L. Madray died in Dorchester County, South Carolina. Louis Madray died in Asheville, North Carolina. How the two women came to live on Nassau Street is a mystery, but Keating and Susan were living in Charleston in 1910. Madray was employed by the railroad at the time. Neither woman was employed at any time during their residence here. Eunice died in Charleston in 1943. The fate of Susan is unknown.

From 1944 through 1969, the house was occupied by a series of tenants who only stayed for a year or two. They were small and large families. They earned their living working in such occupations as a painter, a mechanic, a boiler maker and at the Cigar Factory.

25 Sheppard Street

As the first occupants of 25 Sheppard Street, Thomas and Margaret Whalen lived there from 1910 through 1912. Thomas was born in North Carolina in 1874 and worked as a pipe fitter. Margaret was from Maryland and born in 1870. They were married in 1906. This was his first marriage and her third. Who Margaret was married to previously and what happened to them is unknown. According to the census records, she did have three children. None of the children were living with the Whalens in 1910, so presumably they were from one of Margaret's previous marriages.

The cottage was vacant for unknown reasons for most of the 1920s. For the 1910s and 1930s, it was occupied by a series of families and widows who occupied the house for one to three years at a time. They were employed as clerks, carpenters and by the navy yard.

The longest resident of this cottage was Rachel C. Murray (sometimes Annie C. or Annie R. Murray), widow of Emmanuel D. Murray, who died in Charleston in 1932. Mrs. Murray occupied 25 Sheppard Street from 1938 through 1958. Mrs. Murray was employed by the WPA as a seamstress and a "handicrafts worker" from 1936 through 1940, and then at Charleston Linen Service. She also took in boarders to help make ends meet. Because of the confusion with her name, she is difficult to find with any certainty in the census records, therefore no other information can be found.

The first African American family to occupy this house was James Mitchell and his wife Isabelle. They were a family of seven who occupied the house in at least 1961 but were gone by 1968. No other information can be found about this family.

27 Sheppard Street

William B. Jenkins and his wife, Theodora, occupied 27 Sheppard Street from 1910 through 1912. William and Theodora were both born in South Carolina in 1882 and 1887, respectively. They were married in 1901 and had three children when they moved into this house. The children were Edward (b. 1902), Myrtle (b. 1904) and Johnnie (b. 1906). William was employed by the railroad as a brakeman in 1910 and later as a conductor. By 1920, the family was living in Sumter, South Carolina. They eventually moved to Rutherford, North Carolina, where William died in 1939. The fate of his wife is unknown.

For the next decade, the cottage was home to five different families or individuals. They were employed by the United States Navy, a mill, at the naval yard and as a moulder (shapes sand into molten metal). For much of the 1920s, the cottage was vacant, and William A. Sykes and his family began renting the house in 1930. Sykes was born in 1898 in Florida. He married Lucille L. Warren in 1917 in Charleston County. Lucille was from South Carolina and born in 1899. By 1930, when they moved into this cottage, they had five children. Their children were Dorothy L. (b. 1919), William M. (b. 1921), Evelyn M. (b. 1924), Alfred E. (b. 1928) and Frances H. (b. 1930).

Sykes was employed as a fireman for the City of Charleston. They remained in the house through 1934, and then moved to America Street.

For the next three decades, the house was again occupied by transient families and individuals. There were single men, couples and large and small families who resided in the house. No one stayed longer than a year or two. They held various occupations, skilled and unskilled, such as a carpenter and a painter, and those who worked for the Cigar Factory and the WPA. At no time through 1961 was the house owner-occupied or occupied by African Americans.

29 Sheppard Street

Number 29 Sheppard Street was occupied initially by Henley Hutchinson and his wife, Mary E., with five of their children. The entire family was born in South Carolina. Hutchinson was born in 1872, and worked as a foreman for the railroad. Mary was his second wife, who he married in 1884. They had eight children total, with only six surviving in 1910. The children were Sender L. (b. 1895), Heirman (b. 1898), Rufus (b. 1900), Dorothy (1903) and Carrie B. (b. 1905). What happened to this family after they left Sheppard Street is unknown.

For the next decade, the house was occupied by a string of individuals and small families that stayed for a year or two. They were employed by the railroad, and as carpenters and plumbers. Some were unemployed, and one widow lived there in 1912. The house was then vacant for much of the 1920s, only to resume much of the same in the 1930s, when it was home to a wide variety of short-term tenants.

In 1938, the house was occupied by a large number of individuals. They included Mrs. Mabel Davis and her four children; Mrs. Della Kline, widow of Hampton Kline; and Henry Kline, who was employed by the WPA. That is an amazing number of individuals to fit into a two-room house! How these people were related is unknown. In 1940, Mrs. Davis's husband, James, returned to the house, and was employed by the WPA. Davis died in 1941, and Mabel remained in the house with their children through 1945.

An Architectural Tradition

22 Line Street

The earliest occupants of number 22 Line Street were Benjamin F. Peters and his wife, Clara Belle. Both were born in South Carolina, Benjamin in 1875 and Clara in 1882. They were married in 1906 and had one child, Hellen (b. 1909), at the time they moved into the house. Peters was employed by Southern Railroad as a carpenter and as a flagman. They lived at 22 Line Street from 1910 through 1912, and then relocated 109 Nassau Street for two years. After living in this neighborhood, the Peters family moved to Bogard Street and then to King Street by 1917. In 1919, Clara Peters resided alone according to the city directory and was not a widow. Peters did complete a draft registration card for World War I, so it is possible he was called to duty. However, no other records can be found to substantiate that.

From 1913 through 1938, this cottage was occupied by a variety of short-term tenants. All of them were white, low- to middle-income families and individuals who only stayed in the house for a year, sometimes two. Most of the occupants were employed in skilled professions in such occupations as engineers, a stone cutter, conductors and carpenters.

In 1940, Melvin Barrineau and his family began renting 22 Line Street. Melvin was employed in various capacities related to shipbuilding during the time he and his family occupied the house. Little information can be found regarding this family. Melvin married Carrie Lou (Martin) in 1933. By 1951, the last recorded year they occupied this house, they had three children. No other information can be found.

In 1955, Mrs. Jessie Hale, widow of Jessie L. Hale, occupied the house with her children. Her husband died the year before and was a construction worker. Mrs. Hale was employed as a nurse's aid and had two minor children to provide for. Lula M. Hale lived in the house with them and worked for White Swan Laundry. No other information can be found about this family. Number 22 Line Street is not listed in the city directories after 1955 and through 1970.

28 Line Street (formerly 26 Line Street)

The first occupants of 28 Line Street were two couples who stayed in the house for only one year. William G. Smith and his wife, Della, and John R. Haynes and his wife, Lila, occupied the cottage in 1910. Both of the men worked for the street railway—William as a conductor and John as a motorman. John and Della Haynes were both born in South Carolina, married in 1898 and had one child, although not living with them at that time. The Smiths were also both born in South Carolina, but were married only one year and had no children. The fate of either of these couples after they left Line Street is unknown.

One of the largest families to occupy either cottage on Line Street was the Murrays. John J. Murray and his wife, Mattie, began renting 28 Line Street in 1917, and remained there through 1921. John and Mattie were both born in South Carolina, John in 1881 and Mattie in 1882. John was a carpenter, and was employed at the navy yard at least in 1920. The date and location of their marriage is unknown. By 1920, they had six children—Clifford (b. 1904), Ina M. (b. 1907), Bessie (b. 1909), Ida (b. 1915), Elsie (b. 1918) and a new baby only two months old. After they left Line Street, the family moved to Sumter Street and John went to work for the railroad.

Another large family to occupy the house was the Veno family. Presumably this is the same family of the Dennis Veno who lived at 107 Nassau Street in the 1950s. The Venos were farmers who relocated to Charleston from Berkeley County around 1924 and began renting this cottage. The family consisted of Olin E. Veno and his wife, Louisa, along with their children and Olin's mother, Elther (sometimes Eleather). The entire family was born in South Carolina. Olin was born in 1876 and Louisa in 1885. They had six children by 1920—Dennis (b. 1906), Mary (b. 1908), Mattie (b. 1910), Darden (b. 1912), Louie (b. 1916) and Laurance (b. 1919). Olin's mother was born in 1844. In 1924, not a single member of the family was employed. By 1926, three of the children had unspecified employment with various companies within the city. They only lived at 28 Line Street through 1926, and then relocated to Meeting Street.

For the next decade, the house was occupied by a series of renters employed in various labor-intensive occupations, such as a carpenter and a steamfitter. One occupant was S.D. Harrelson, who was listed as an employee of the Cooper River Bridge in 1929. Presumably that means he was hired as part of the workforce that constructed the bridge.

In 1938, the first African Americans occupied the house. Ella Frasier and her two children moved into 28 Line Street. She was employed by the Cigar Factory and lived in the house on and off through 1951. At the same time, Nathaniel Parker and/or Ella Parker lived in the house on and off from 1940 through 1945. It is unclear how they were related or if Ella is really only one person. No other records can be found regarding the three names.

After Ella Frasier left the house in 1951, Joseph Bradley and his wife, Ella F., occupied the house through 1958. They, too, were African Americans. Joseph worked for the City of Charleston and the State Ports Authority. No other information can be found regarding this couple.

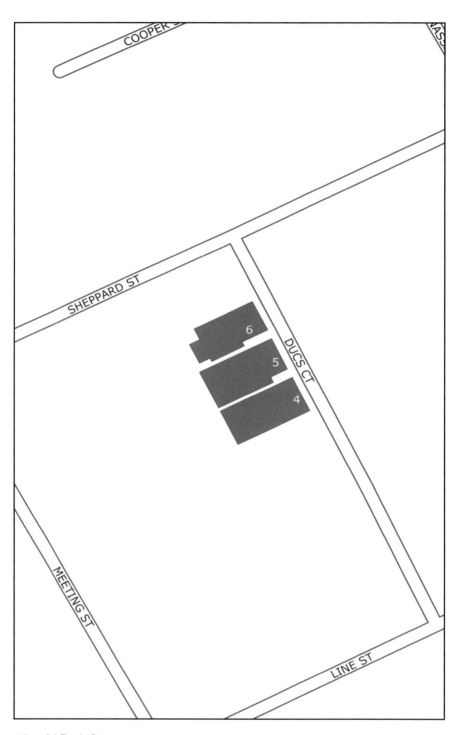

4,5 and 6 Duc's Court.

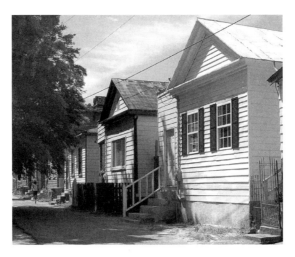

4, 5 and 6 Duc's Court, with number 6 in the foreground.

4, 5 AND 6 DUC'S COURT

Duc's Court is a small alley that runs north–south between Sheppard and Line Streets in the block between Nassau and Meeting Streets. Records about this block are scant, but it appears that these three cottages were constructed before 1882. There were four single-story wood-frame dwellings and three two-story wood-frame dwellings built on the west side of this narrow alley, and none on the east. Construction of the buildings was commissioned by Henry Alex Duc Sr. Duc was a tinner (sheet metal worker, or sometimes a roofer) born in South Carolina in 1815 to French-immigrant parents. He and his wife, Emma, resided on Spring Street and raised four children—Perscilla (b. 1845), Edward (b. 1847), Henry S. (b. 1849) and Lawrance (b. 1853). Duc died in 1892 from influenza and the property passed to his grandson, Henry A. Duc Jr., born in 1866. Duc followed in his grandfather's footsteps and worked as a tinner as well. Because of the size of the Duc family, and the fact that they had many similar names, it was difficult to trace their genealogy with certainty. It appears that Henry Duc Jr. never married. He held large swaths of property in this area and rented out the cottages until selling all of it off in pieces to Ishum F. Lanier between 1907 and 1911. He died in the emergency hospital in Washington, D.C., in 1920. He left the majority of his estate to be split between four friends who were employed by the Continental Iron Works in Brooklyn, New York. He left portions of his estate to charities such as the Colored Orphan Asylum and the Society for the Prevention of Cruelty to Animals, both in Charleston. He also left a dollar to each of his nieces and nephews with specific instructions on how they were to prove they were related to him.

These dwellings were rarely ever owner-occupied. One member of the Duc family lived on Duc's Court in the 1880s, but lived at 8 Duc's Court, which was a two-story dwelling. None of these three cottages was ever owner-occupied until the 1950s. Number 4 was occupied by its owner for one year in 1950–51. Number 5 was owner-occupied after it was purchased in 1952, and remains so. Number 6 was never owner-occupied.

The occupants of the houses between 1905 and 1929 are largely unknown, as the addresses in this alley were not listed in the city directories for that time period, but some of the years could be filled in using the census in conjunction with the directories. For the years that the occupants are known, there were primarily low- to middle-income white individuals and families living in these structures. The properties seemed to attract an inordinate number of immigrants and widows.

The physical form of these buildings is similar to the ones constructed by Ishum Lanier. Originally they were constructed as the typical two-room linear dwelling with a piazza running the full length of the south elevation. By 1920, Lanier had modified them with an addition at the southwest corner, enclosing the rear portion of the piazza. Since 1920, each of these cottages has been modified additionally, with more piazza enclosures, rear additions and changes to the details. The piazza was filled in on 4 Duc's Court and a small addition constructed to the rear of the piazza. The roof was likely replaced as well. The other two have gable roofs (as do all the other houses on the street commissioned by Henry A. Duc) and number 4 has a low-sloped hip roof. Number 5 was heavily modified in the 1950s, with a large picture window replacing the original windows, and the piazza balustrade and columns were replaced with wrought iron. In 1985, number 6 was the most intact of all three structures. It still had its turned balusters and columns on the piazza and a very ornate door surround on the piazza screen. Since that time, most of the details have been removed and the entire piazza screen was reconstructed without the beautiful door surround.

An Architectural Tradition

4 Duc's Court

The first known occupant of this cottage was John Andrea Lilienthal, who lived in the house from 1886 through 1892. Lilienthal was a carpenter, born in Germany in 1865. The year he immigrated to the United States is unknown. He married Anna Friede Theiling of Charleston in 1885, who was born in 1867 of German parents. They had a total of eight children together, but had lost five of them by 1910. They had two sons and a daughter between the ages of fourteen and nineteen, whose names appeared in the census as initials only. All three children were employed in 1910. One son was a framer, the other was making cigars and their daughter was a bookbinder. No information can be found regarding the fate of this family after 1910.

The next tenants in the house were James O'Neal Beattie (sometimes Beatty) and his wife, Bessie (Langan). The Beatties resided in the house from 1894 through 1898. James was born in Florida in 1859. While they lived on Duc's Court, Beattie was employed by the South Carolina and Georgia Railroad as a blacksmith. Bessie was born in Ireland in 1870, and immigrated to the United States in 1883. The couple was married in Charleston County in 1891. They had seven children, only two of whom lived in this house. Their children were John F. (b. 1893), James (b. 1896), Ruth (b. 1899), Julian (b. 1901), Anthony (b. 1904), Mary (b. 1906) and Blanche (b. 1910). After the family left Duc's Court, they resided nearby on Nassau Street until around 1920, when they relocated to Berkeley County, South Carolina. James died in 1936 in Charleston. The fate of his wife is unknown.

The next known occupants to stay in the house for more than a year were Arthur and Kate Thompson. They lived in the cottage from 1910 through 1912. Arthur and Kate were both born in South Carolina in 1880. They had four children together, three of whom died very early in their lives. Their surviving daughter, Ada, was born in 1900 and lived at 4 Duc's Court with them. Arthur was employed by the Atlantic Coast Line Railroad as a brakeman and a car inspector.

The rest of the known occupants of the house only stayed there one to two years. The majority of the tenants were white individuals and families. The family sizes ranged from single people to families of nine! They worked in such professions as laborers, a pipe fitter, carpenters, salesmen and in the Cigar Factory. Between 1930 and 1940, four different widows and their children occupied the residence. In the 1950s, ownership of the parcel changed, and it appears to have been owner-occupied at least one year. In 1950, it was purchased by James B. Orvin, who also occupied the cottage that year. The city directories indicate that one James O. Boyd occupied the house the rest of the decade, but James B. Orvin continued to have ownership. James O. Boyd cannot be found in the "resident directory" portion of the directories so this may represent typographical errors, in which case it was owner-occupied for much of the entire decade. No further information can be found about either one of these names. Starting in 1965, the Just family owned and occupied the house. Theirs was a large family of nine (or more). Harry Just was employed as a cook at the Citadel. The property remained in the Just family's possession on and off through the year 2000.

5 Duc's Court

For reasons that are unclear, this dwelling was vacant for many years in the 1880s and 1890s. The earliest known resident was Van A. Iseman, for which little information can be found. It is known that he was a white man who worked as a driver. He lived in the house in 1891 and 1892. He cannot be found in any other records before or after that time period. The house was not occupied again until 1899, when it was occupied by Richard and Isabella Williams. Richard worked for the South Carolina and Georgia Railroad as a carpenter. They only lived in the house for one year.

Arthur J. Hemmingway and his wife, Ella, lived at 5 Duc's Court the following year. Hemmingway was born in South Carolina in 1844, and Ella in 1870. They had four children, only two of whom survived—two sons born in 1893 and 1896. Hemmingway worked as a machinist and the family took in a boarder to help make ends meet. The fate of this family after 1900 is unknown.

The recorded tenants that followed over the next two decades were much of the same. They only stayed for a year or two and worked in local factories, for the city or for the railroad. In 1931, the Bunch family began renting the house. Minnie Bunch and her four daughters—Pearl (b. 1915), Bessie (b. 1905), Mae or Mary (b. 1909) and Thelma (b. 1912)—moved to Charleston after the death of her husband, Thomas. Thomas and Minnie were uneducated white farmers living in Orangeburg, South Carolina, until

Thomas died in 1930, at the age of forty-eight. Minnie and her daughters possibly moved to be near Minnie's mother, Mary Kelly, who was living next door at 4 Duc's Court. All of the women in both houses were employed at the Cigar Factory. The extended family lived next door to each other for two years, and then relocated to other houses in the neighborhood.

Thaddeus J. Mazzell and his wife, Estell, began renting the house in 1938. It appears that they had at least five children living with them when they moved into this tiny structure. All of their names and dates of birth cannot be determined. In 1930, they had four children and were residing on America Street with Thaddeus's brother and his family. The children were Clifford (b. 1923), Lucile (b. 1925), Hilton (b. 1927) and Paul (b. 1929). Mazzell was born in South Carolina in 1895. He was a machinist at either the Cigar Factory or in a candy factory. Estell was also born in South Carolina, but in 1897. Estell disappears from the records altogether after 1942, and Thaddeus died in 1944 while living in Charleston.

For the next six years, the house continued to be used for rental purposes. In 1952, Wilhelmina Jones purchased the property and moved in, presumably with her husband. She then became the first African American occupant and the first owner-occupant as well. Not much can be found regarding Mrs. Jones. She was born Wilhelmenia White and married Louis O. Jones in Charleston County in 1938. Louis was born in 1918. He never graduated from high school and enlisted in the military during WWII at the age of twenty-five. Louis died sometime between 1961 and 1968. Mrs. Jones was employed as a cook after the death of her husband. Mrs. Jones continues to reside in the house and retain ownership of the parcel.

6 Duc's Court

The cottage at 6 Duc's Court has a similar history as the neighboring houses, but only slightly better documented. The first documented occupant is Archibald J. Gary in 1892. He only occupied the house that one year while working in a barrel factory. Whether or not this gentleman is related to the Archie J. Garry of 36 Sheppard Street at the turn of the century is unknown. For the rest of the decade the house was occupied by a series of white tenants employed in such capacities as a driver for the city railway, a clerk and a carpenter.

In 1900, James W. Bean and his wife, Maggie (Roscher), moved into the house from Spring Street. Bean was born in Ireland in 1870, and his wife was born in Georgia in 1875. They were married in 1892 in Charleston County and had seven children—John (b. 1893), Willie (b. 1896), Ethel (b. 1898), Joseph (b. 1900), Mary (b. 1904) and Margaret (b. 1910). Sadly, John Bean died in the house on New Year's Eve 1902, at the tender age of nine. He was playing with a toy pistol when a cap exploded in his finger. He died from tetanus.

The Beans stayed in the house through 1904 before moving to Reid Street. James was employed in a wide variety of occupations in Charleston. He worked as a policeman in Hampton Park on and off, and also as a salesman, a clerk and a farmer. Likely for health reasons, the Bean family eventually relocated to the town of Summerville, where James succumbed to tuberculosis in 1913, at the age of forty-five.

From 1909 through 1911, Alvertis (or Albert) and Fannie Mizell occupied the house with their five children. Their children were Lessie (b. 1898), Robert (b. 1901), Mandi (b. 1904), Samuel (b. 1905) and Alberta (b. 1902). Albert and Fannie were both born in South Carolina in 1873. They were married at the age of twenty-three in 1896. Albert worked as a house carpenter. In 1912, they left Duc's Court to live on Cooper Street.

In 1931, George W. Craven and his family moved into the cottage. Some member of the Craven family stayed in the house longer than any other tenants in these three houses combined. The Cravens relocated to this house after many years of farming in Colleton County, and then in St. Andrews (Charleston County). The entire family was born in South Carolina. George was born in either 1858 or 1865. His wife, Janie, was born in 1877. They had at least ten children together—nine of whom survived through 1930. In 1930, their children were Edna (b. 1900), Ashley (b. 1904), Ivy (b. 1906), Isabelle (b. 1914), Virgie (b. 1917), Lessie (b. 1918), Ruby (b. 1922), Jim (b. 1924) and George (b. 1926). George Sr. died in 1932, just a short time after moving to Charleston. He left his wife with five minor children to provide for. Janie and the children stayed in the house through 1945. Oftentimes her son Ivy lived in the house with them, presumably to help make ends meet. He and several of his siblings were employed by the Cigar Factory.

In the late 1940s, the house was owner-occupied for the first time by Edward and Melwood Murray. They sold the property in 1952, and it again reverted to investment property. From that point through the 1960s, it was home to a variety of African Americans and their families. One such example is Newman F. Omega and his wife, Louise, who moved in around 1961. Newman was a Methodist pastor. They had three young children living with them and were gone from the house by 1968. Between 1980 and 2004, this parcel changed hands eight times, with the majority of those transactions occurring between 1997 and 2004.

PART IV

THE UPPER PENINSULA

North of Line Street and South of Mount Pleasant Street

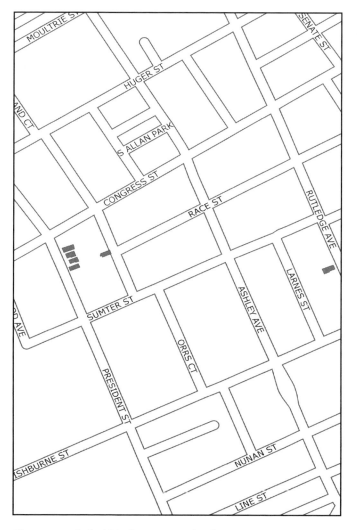

Cottages studied within the upper peninsula.

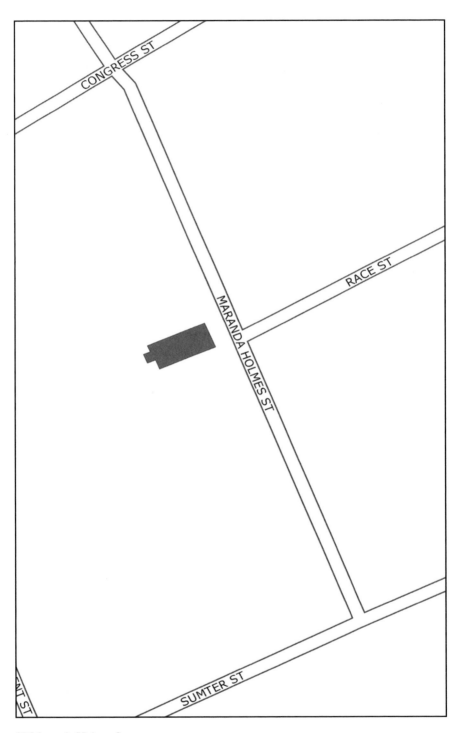

23 Maranda Holmes Street.

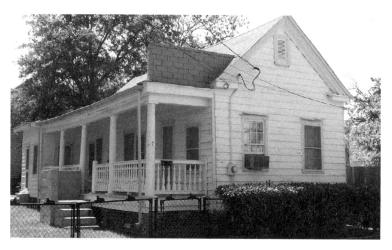

23 Maranda Holmes Street.

23 MARANDA HOLMES STREET
(FORMERLY 7 COURT STREET)

Maranda Holmes Street is a small, narrow street that runs between Sumter and Congress Streets. It was renamed from Court Street in 2006. The street was named in honor of a former resident of the street who had lived there for sixty-four years. Maranda Holmes was an advocate for the poor and has been referred to as one of Court Street's "porch mothers." The history of this particular cottage is more typical of the folklore surrounding these buildings. It *was* constructed by and occupied by African Americans exclusively. It was owner-occupied in its early history, but only by the family responsible for its construction. After 1912, it was never owner-occupied again; oddly, however, it did not experience the high turnover of tenants that these houses typically did when used for investment purposes. Tenants tended to stay for long periods of time. Today it sits vacant and somewhat dilapidated, with its windows shuttered.

This cottage is located on the east side of the street and was constructed in 1883. According to the tax records, this house was "rebuilt" between 1894 and 1898, but there is no break in occupancy to substantiate that information. Construction was commissioned by Boston Sweeper, a formerly enslaved African American born in 1844 in South Carolina. Sweeper's life was relatively short, but full. At the age of twenty-one, Sweeper enlisted in the military, serving as a private for nineteen months, from March 1865 through October 1866. He was discharged due to consumption (tuberculosis). By

1878, Sweeper was living on Court Street in Charleston and working as a laborer. During the time Sweeper resided in Charleston, he held various unskilled, labor-intensive jobs, such as a farmhand, a gravedigger and a sexton (person in charge of the maintenance of church buildings and/or the surrounding graveyard).

Although the exact date of their marriage is unknown, it appears that Sweeper married Binah in 1897 or 1898, when she first appears in the city directories as his wife. Little is known about Binah other than she was born in South Carolina in 1861, and it is likely that she was married previously.

Sweeper finally succumbed to his tuberculosis in the house in August 1899, at the age of fifty-five. He left his wife to care for three young girls—Emma (b. 1886), Ella (b. 1896) and Eallie (b. 1892). Sweeper bequeathed 7 Court Street to his wife, specifying that it be passed to his "adopted" daughter, Emma, after Binah's death. The other daughters were not mentioned in the will.

Binah and/or her daughters remained in the house through 1912, and the property remained in the family's possession until 1919. Records regarding the Sweeper family are scant, so it is difficult to understand what happened to Binah and her daughters after 1912. However, when the property was sold in 1919, it was by Emma Sweeper Smiley, which would indicate that Binah had already died. The cause and location of her death cannot be determined. Between 1912 and 1919, the house was occupied by tenants.

In 1913, Samuel S. Brinton and his wife, Catharine (Wright), moved into the house as the first tenants and remained there through 1920. The Brintons married in 1903 in Charleston County. Samuel was born in South Carolina in 1850, and worked as a laborer at odd jobs. Catharine, also of South Carolina, was born in 1858. This appears to have been a second marriage for each of them. In 1900, Samuel was living at 13 Court Street ("Short Court"). He was a widower with three children—John (b. 1881), Edward (b. 1886) and Amelia (b. 1884). By 1910, Catharine is said to have only one surviving child of four, Jessie Cullender (b. 1900). The other three children were likely from this previous marriage as well. Samuel died at the age of sixty-eight in 1918, leaving Catharine to fend for herself as a "huckster" (retail merchant or peddler of wares).

The tenants who resided in the house the longest were Reverend Franklin R. Young and his wife Amanda (Brunson). They moved into the house in 1925, and had at least two children, Ida (b. 1919) and Frank Jr. (DOB unknown). It appears that Ida died very young, as she disappears from the records almost immediately. Not much can be found about Franklin Young. He was born in South Carolina in 1873, and was a "clergyman" or "presiding elder" at "Charleston A.M.E. Church." Mrs. Young was twenty years younger than her husband. She was one of seven children born to Julius and Ida Brunson in Sumter, South Carolina, in 1893. Brunson was a farmer. Reverend Young died in 1941. His wife and son remained in the house through 1948, and then moved from the city.

By 1950, Ophelia Smalls was living in the house as a tenant. Very little information can be found about her other than she was a single, African American woman employed as a maid. She remained in the house until her death in 1963.

This cottage, while it is vacant and in need of repair, continues to retain much of its original fabric and character. It has undergone very few alterations. The house survived the earthquake of 1886 relatively intact. The chimneys cracked all the way to their foundations and were supposed to have been rebuilt. Whether or not this ever happened is unknown. At some point all the chimneys were removed. A small rear addition was constructed in the late twentieth century, concrete block steps were added to access the piazza and the foundation was altered, probably all during the same time frame.

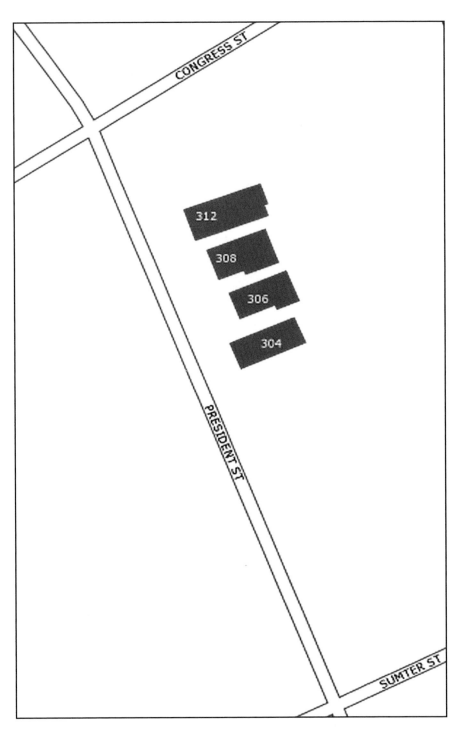

304–312 President Street.

304, 306, 308 AND 312 PRESIDENT STREET

These four adjacent cottages are located on the east side of President Street, between Sumter and Congress Streets. They were all constructed within a few years of each other, but by different property owners. The land was subdivided by James W. Fraser (sometimes "Frasier") in 1909, and subsequently sold over the next few years. There are a few conflicts in the records about who actually owned the land during the time of construction. It would appear that at least one of the cottages (306) was commissioned and likely constructed by Fraser himself.

Fraser was an African American (sometimes referred to as "mulatto") contractor born in South Carolina around 1870. He married Catherine Gourdin in 1898, and had a very large family. When the Frasers were first married, they resided with Catherine's parents and siblings on F Street in Charleston. By 1910, they owned and lived at 73 Spring Street with their six children, Catherine's mother and three of Catherine's siblings. By 1920, they had had three more children and several of Catherine's family members continued to reside in the house. Their children were Anna G. (b. 1898), James W. Jr. (b. 1902), Catherine E. (b. 1904), Marguerite A. (b. 1905), Carry E. (b. 1907), Emily E. (b. 1910), Mary J. (b. 1913), Helen V. (b. 1916) and Ruth L. (b. 1919). Fraser died in 1923, leaving his widow to care for this family alone. Catherine survived her husband by thirty-two years.

Fraser died with an estate appraised at $39,000. He owned sixty parcels of land in the city, with most of it being in the upper peninsula on Carolina,

Fishburne and Sumter Streets. He named his wife executrix and asked that the estate stay intact to support her and any children through 1930. At that time, she was to take possession of one-third of the estate and divide the rest up between any surviving children. All of this was null and void if Catherine remarried. The estate was not settled until 1944.

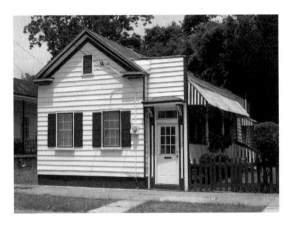

304 President Street.

304 President Street

The construction of 304 President Street was commissioned in 1911 by Julia (Robinson) Saunders. She purchased the parcel prior to marrying Burrell Saunders. They were married by 1915, but the exact date and location is unknown. Julia was African American and born in South Carolina in 1888. Her name does not appear in many documents so her life was difficult to trace. It is known that she ended up living in Manhattan with her husband and some extended family by at least 1930. Burrell Saunders, also African American, was born in Virginia in 1879, and was employed as an engineer. He resided in Manhattan for most of his adult life and was a widower by 1910, making Julia his second wife. The couple did not appear to have any children except for one adopted daughter, Bernice Holder (b. 1922). They continued to reside in Manhattan through 1942, when they disappear from the records entirely.

Rosa Grant purchased this cottage from Julia Saunders in 1915, but was already living in the house with her husband, Adam, by 1914. The property exchanged hands for "five dollars and other valuable considerations." The nature of the relationship between the Grants and Julia Robinson is unknown, but given the purchase price, it must have been of a personal nature. Adam Grant was an African American, born in South Carolina in 1875. Throughout his life, Grant was employed in odd jobs, such as a driver and a laborer. His wife, also of South Carolina, was born in 1870. The date of their marriage is unknown, but by 1900 they had four daughters—Julia (b. 1888), Ida (b. 1889), Viola (b. 1893) and Martha (b. 1895). In 1900, they were living with another family at 5 Court Street (next door to Binah Sweeper and her daughters), which, incidentally, was another freedman's cottage that the Grants had constructed in 1883.

One month after purchasing 304 President Street, the Grants sold it to Oliveros W. Kroeg. Again the property was sold for "five dollars and other valuable considerations." Again, their relationship is unknown, but certainly of a personal nature. The Grants remained as residents of the cottage through 1917, and then moved out of the city. After the sale in 1915, the property went through a series of owners and occupants, being used predominantly as investment property until 1936. During this time, with the exception of one year, it was occupied by African American families and individuals employed as laborers, painters and hucksters. There was relatively low turnover in residents over time. Between 1916 and 1930, six different families lived in the house.

The family that lived there the longest during that time period was David and Julia O'Neill, who also owned the property. O'Neill was born in South Carolina in 1883. He worked as porter and a laborer while living in the house with his wife from 1920 until he died in 1924. When O'Neill died, he left his wife to care for an eleven-year-old son, John. Apparently, after his death, Julia O'Neill was unable to keep up payments on the property as it was sold at auction in October 1924. Julia then appears to have left the city. No records can be found as to what happened to her or her son after 1924.

In 1930, Reverend Samuel Lloyd and his wife, Edith, moved into the house and six years later, they purchased the property from the real estate company, W.C. Wilbur & Company. Lloyd was an African American pastor at St. Luke's Reformed Episcopal Church at 60 Nassau Street. How long he served there is unknown. Lloyd was born in 1884 in South Carolina. By 1910, he was a student of theology in some unspecified seminary, but was a resident of the city of Charleston. By 1920, he was married, living on Bull Street and employed as a pastor. By 1930, he and his wife had a ten-year-old adopted son, Frank Perry. There is no record of them having any other children. Lloyd died intestate in 1937, leaving twenty-one heirs. Edith lived in the house until 1977, and died in 1978 in Mount Pleasant. At this time, all of the heirs agreed to convey their interest in 304 President Street to

Mrs. Lloyd. It then passed to Frank Perry Lloyd, the Lloyds' adopted son. The property remains in the possession of the Lloyd family and is used for investment purposes.

This house has undergone very few alterations and retains its original character and charm. A portion of the piazza has been enclosed and there is a rear addition with a shed roof. The date of these elements is unknown. It is known that the current owner has taken pains to keep the house the way it was when her grandparents (Samuel and Edith Lloyd) owned it.

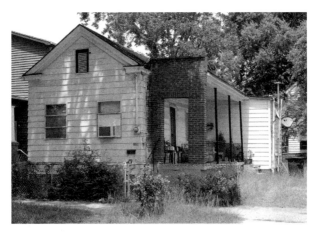

306 President Street.

306 President Street

The construction of this cottage was commissioned by James W. Fraser in 1912. Fraser sold the property to Julia Saunders in 1915, who in turn conveyed it to John C. Carter in February 1918 for "ten dollars and other valuable considerations." Carter was born in South Carolina in 1881. He married Henrietta Drayton, also of South Carolina, in 1900, and worked as a laborer at the navy yard. This family certainly had its share of heartache. In the first ten years of their marriage, they experienced the loss of three children. The circumstances of their deaths are unknown. By the time the Carters moved into 306 President Street in 1918, they were a family of five with one more on the way. Their children were Ruth (b. 1908), John (b. 1910), Alberta (b. 1915) and Agnes (b. 1918 or 1919). Six months after moving into the house, Carter died at the age of thirty-six from influenza and pneumonia, leaving his pregnant widow with five young children to care for.

John Carter died intestate, so the property transferred to his wife and children. Henrietta and the children remained in the house through 1925, and then moved out of the city. In 1930, Henrietta resided with her daughter, Ruth, and family in Yonkers, New York. By 1954, Henrietta was remarried and known as Henrietta Carter Wilkenson.

In 1954, Henrietta and the children sold the property to Freda Doscher. Doscher rented out the house until she sold it to Jonathan Riley in 1956. During the time period after the Carters left the house and it sold in 1956, the house was occupied by low- to middle-income African Americans who stayed only for a year or two at a time. Many had no occupations listed in the city directories, but others were carpenters, laborers, truck drivers and a nurse, to name a few. The house was not owner-occupied after the Carters left until 1956, when the Rileys purchased the property. Riley, who was an African American truck driver, lived there with his wife, J'Metta, and children through 1983, when it was purchased by the current owners.

This cottage has undergone a great deal of alterations, particularly in the 1950s and '60s. The entire piazza, except the roof, was replaced, as were the windows. An addition to the rear and a partial piazza enclosure were completed as well.

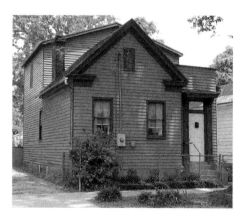

308 President Street.

308 President Street

The parcel where 308 President Street stands was purchased in 1909 by Paul Blocker from James W. Fraser. Blocker did not have a house constructed on the lot for about six years after purchasing it. Just prior to construction,

Blocker sold one half interest to his wife for one dollar. During the time between purchasing the property and constructing the house, he and his wife, Binah (Richardson?), resided on Race Street, and Paul worked as a laborer. Paul was born in South Carolina in 1868, and his wife was born in 1865. They married in 1903.

In 1910, while they were still living on Race Street, they also had (John) Eugene Richardson (b. 1889), Binah's son from a previous marriage, and Eugene Richardson Jr. (b. 1902) living with them. This census indicates that Eugene Richardson had been married for four years, but his wife is not listed as part of the family. Also according to the census, Richardson and Blocker were both employed by a mill as laborers in 1910. This information conflicts with information found in other records.

Eugene Richardson and Lily (Rivers) were married in 1906 and were living on Race Street as early as 1908. He was employed as a butcher at that time. They remained on Race Street and Eugene was employed by the same company through 1914; however, Lily was no longer listed as his wife after 1912. No records can be found as to the fate of Lily. In 1916, Eugene and his new wife, Mary (Jackson), were living at 215 St. Philip Street. Eugene continued to be employed as a butcher with the same company.

The 1910 census also indicates that Binah had four children, with only three still living, but no records can be found as to who or where they were in 1910. In 1916, the Blockers moved into their new house at 308 President Street, but the makeup of the family at that time is unknown. Richardson's World War I draft card of 1917 indicates that he was living at 225 St. Philip Street and was the sole provider for his wife, child and mother. Presumably this means his mother-in-law as he, his wife Mary, and his mother-in-law were living at 225 St. Philip Street in 1920. The whereabouts of Eugene Jr. are unknown. It does not appear that they had any other children.

In November 1931, Paul died in the house of pneumonia and intestinal blockage. Binah remained there until 1935, and then died in 1936, at the age of sixty (from "paralysis," presumably a stroke). The property was then sold to Edward Smith.

Smith was an African American tinner who lived in the house with his wife, Elizabeth, and their child through 1945. In 1954, Elizabeth Smith sold the property to Bernard and Ethel Deas who had been renting the house since at least 1948. Deas, also African American, was a letter carrier for the United States Post Office. The Deas family held the property until 1989. During much of that time, Mrs. Smith continued to reside in the house on and off. The relationship between the Deas family and Smiths is unknown. Number 308 President Street seems to be a bit of an anomaly in that the number of occupants over time is far fewer than most of the cottages studied.

Number 308 President Street was modified extensively in the mid- to late twentieth century with a large two-story addition at the rear. It seems that a portion of the original house was removed to accommodate this addition. The columns on the piazza were replaced with ones influenced by the Craftsman style.

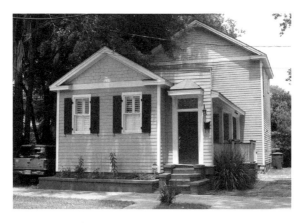

312 President Street.

312 President Street

312 President Street was constructed in 1912, and commissioned by John S. and Daisy Bell Johnson. The parcel was purchased in Mrs. Johnson's name the previous year from T.W. Weston. The Johnsons were an African American (sometimes referred to as "mulatto") couple who were both born in South Carolina. John was born in 1877 and Daisy in 1890, as Daisy Bell Glover. The couple was married in Charleston County in October 1907, and it does not appear that they had any children. John worked as a house painter and Daisy was a dressmaker. In the 1920s, Daisy was the treasurer and secretary for an organization known as the United Order of Easter Gates. Unfortunately, no information can be found regarding this organization. The couple moved into the house immediately after construction and stayed until they sold the property to John G. Ferguson in 1929. The fate of John and Daisy Johnson after they moved from President Street is unknown.

The property remained in Ferguson's possession until 1975. During all that time, he never occupied the residence, but rented it out to a wide variety of African American tenants. The first such tenants of his in 1930 were two unrelated African American women, no doubt struggling to survive. One of the women was Rebecca Graham, a forty-year-old widow (of Henry Graham, who died that same year) working as a maid for a private family. The other occupants were Bessie Grant and her two children, Elizabeth (b. 1926) and Leon (b. 1927). Bessie worked from home, doing laundry for others. Following these women were a series of low-income African American individuals and families, holding such occupations as a maid, a stevedore, a teacher and a painter. No one occupied the house more than a year or two until William and Elsie Green moved into the house in 1948. William Green was a painter. They had at least one minor child living with them and remained in the house through 1958.

This house underwent an enormous number of alterations during its almost one-hundred-year history. It was originally constructed as the typical two-room rectangular cottage with a south-facing piazza. Throughout the first half of the twentieth century, multiple rear additions were constructed and the footprint of the piazza modified. In 2004, the structure was gutted, many of the historic additions were removed and the rear two-story addition was constructed. Additionally, the front wall of the cottage was reconstructed.

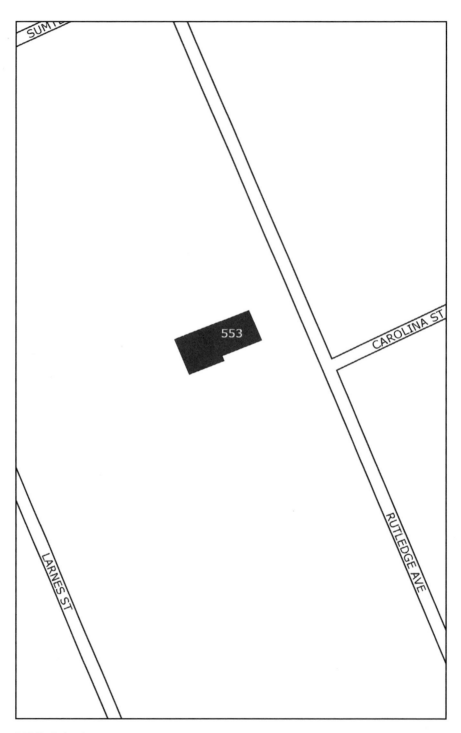

553 Rutledge Avenue.

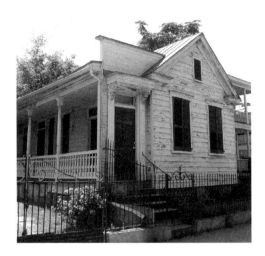

553 Rutledge Avenue.

553 RUTLEDGE AVENUE

Number 553 Rutledge Avenue is located on the west side of the street between Sumter and Fishburne Streets, and has a unique history compared to the other cottages studied for this book. Unlike most of these cottages, the carpenter is known and the building was built for, by and lived in by the same family for over one hundred years. This cottage was constructed in 1903 by George H. Holmes, an African American carpenter. He purchased the lot in February 1903 from Fred A. Peters. The property remained within his family's possession until purchased by the current owner in 2007.

Holmes was born in Charleston on September 15, 1870, to Jefferson and Elsa Holmes. Holmes learned his skills as a carpenter from his father, who was a former slave in Charleston. Holmes was married and had the first of ten children by 1889. His wife, Emma, was born in South Carolina in 1873. Emma gave him five daughters, including a set of twins, and five sons. The children were Henry (b. 1889), Anna (b. 1892), William (b. 1893), Frank (b. 1898), Georgetta and Ernestine (b. 1905), Julius (b. 1907), Mabel (b. 1909), Melvin (b. 1911) and Lillian (b. 1913). Henry died at a very young age, but all the rest of the children were raised in this tiny house. Over time, Holmes modified the original building by constructing additions to the rear to accommodate his large family.

Emma died in 1929, leaving George with two teenage children to raise. George, being unable to work for the last two years of his life, finally succumbed to a long illness in 1935. The parcel passed to his children, some of whom lived in the house on and off throughout the twentieth century. Mabel married John Watson and became a teacher. Julian and Melvin were employed as carpenters or contractors. What happened to the rest of the family is unknown.

Given the fact that the house was occupied by multiple carpenters, it is understandable that it underwent many changes throughout its history. Multiple building campaigns of rear additions happened early in the twentieth century. In 2007, when the property was no longer owned or occupied by a member of the Holmes family, one or more of the rear additions were removed and the whole structure was gutted and renovated.

CONCLUSION

The Charleston "freedman's cottage" has a long and diverse history in the city. It would appear, however, that they have nothing specifically to do with freed slaves as a building type. More aptly described in several instances in the 1980s and '90s, these buildings were merely constructed as "the poor man's Charleston single house." In 1989, Walter B. Hill did extensive research into the life of African Americans in Charleston from 1880 to 1910. These dates coincide nicely with the dates of construction for the majority of the structures researched for this work. His research concluded that during this time period African Americans in Charleston sought places to live based on economics and the availability of land.

Additionally he did discuss the fact that there was generally a great shift in population from the lower peninsula to the upper peninsula, or "the neck," between 1880 and 1910. This shift was largely due to availability of land and economic factors—land was cheaper, rents were lower and controls were more lax in the upper peninsula.

With this influx of population to the upper peninsula came a mix of ethnicities and a great deal of new construction. In the late nineteenth and early twentieth centuries, much of the land in the neck was subdivided from former farms. One such subdivision provides several examples of Charleston single houses (or at least two-story wood-frame houses) being built by and for freed slaves. The area between Race and Congress Streets, west of King Street, was subdivided into twenty-seven lots and auctioned off in 1882. Several parcels on Race Street were purchased by African American families who built their own homes there shortly after purchasing the lots. Number 20

Race Street, a two-story wood-framed structure, was constructed by James W. Gordon. Two structures were built at 21 Race Street, both of which were two-story wood-frame dwellings. They were constructed or commissioned by Catherine and/or Frank Aiken. Number 26½ Race Street was constructed by Henry Chisolm and was also a two-story wood-frame dwelling. All of these houses, and more, were on these lots and occupied by 1883. They are no longer extant, likely replaced by the Greek Orthodox Church and Hellenic Center that were built in the mid-twentieth century.

James Gordon, Frank Aiken and Henry Chisolm were all carpenters and former slaves in South Carolina. The 1900 census indicates that this block of Race Street continued be occupied entirely by African Americans born prior to the end of the Civil War. In all likelihood they were former slaves as well. They lived in a mix of one- and two-story wood-frame houses and not exclusively in so-called "freedman's cottages."

Of the structures studied for this work, several general calculations can be made regarding who commissioned their construction as well as their occupancy. Of the four cottages studied in the lower peninsula, the average date of construction was 1870. They were 50 percent owner-occupied and occupied by African Americans 29 percent of the time. The construction of these dwellings was commissioned by whites as often as African Americans. Of the fourteen cottages studied on the west side, the average date of construction was 1892. They were more often used as rental property than they were owner-occupied, and they were occupied by African Americans 79 percent of the time. The construction of 46 percent of these dwellings was commissioned by African Americans. The statistics for the east side are most surprising as this area has always been considered to be a predominantly African American-occupied area of the city. The average date of construction for these houses was 1901. Not a single one of these dwellings was constructed or commissioned by an African American. They were used for rental purposes about 85 percent of the time and were occupied by African Americans only 25 percent of the time, and that was typically not until the late 1950s. The statistics for the upper peninsula are quite different from the east side. The average date of construction was 1898. They were predominantly used as rental property, especially after their initial construction. They were occupied by African Americans 96 percent of the time. Of the sixteen buildings studied in this area, 64 percent of them were commissioned by African Americans.

Similar to every other house type in the city, the ownership and ethnicity of the occupants of these so-called "freedman's cottages" was more dependent on the demographics of the neighborhood as a whole. There appears to be no truth to the myth that they were constructed by and/or for freed slaves after the Civil War.

This knowledge may bring disappointment to some, and may make the cottages seem less valuable as a building type in the city. However, they are no less valuable now than they were when you started reading this book. Each of the houses has a story to tell—sometimes with drama and sometimes without. However, some of the stories may be similar to your own, or the occupants may be people you can relate to. It is important that these stories (i.e., the cottages) be retained for future generations. These Charleston cottages are becoming rare in this historic city. They remain one of the most undervalued building types in Charleston and should be revered and protected like a dying species. They have their own valuable and interesting tales to tell. This is only the beginning of the story as there is much more work to be done.

BIBLIOGRAPHY

Alston, Elizabeth, Robert P. Stockton, et al. "Information for Guides of Historic Charleston," undated. Unpublished document on file at the Charleston County Library, South Carolina History Room.

Bass, Kenlyn. "A History of a Freedman's Cottage at 40 Morris Street," 2006. Unpublished document on file at the Avery Research Center for African American History and Culture, 125 Bull Street, Charleston, South Carolina.

Behre, Robert. "Habitat Saves House at 11 H Street." *(Charleston) Post and Courier*, May 12, 2003, p. 1-B.

———. "Mysterious Freedman's Cottages Getting New Look." *(Charleston) Post and Courier*, July 24, 2006, p. 1-B.

———. "On the Hunt for Answers About Freedman's Cottages." *(Charleston) Post and Courier*, October 26, 1998, p. 1-B.

Bridges and Allens Map of the City of Charleston, 1852. On file at the Charleston County Library, South Carolina History Room.

California Death Index, 1940–97. http://www.ancestry.com.

Charleston City Directories, 1830–2007. On file at the Charleston County Library, South Carolina History Room.

Charleston County Health Department Death Records, 1819–1926. On file at the Charleston County Public Library, South Carolina History Room.

Charleston County Probate Records (marriage licenses and estate records), 1800–1970. On file with the Charleston County Probate Court and the Charleston County Public Library, South Carolina History Room.

Charleston County RMC Office, plats, deeds and indices, 1800–2008.

Charleston County Ward Books, 1852–1961. On file with the Charleston County Assessor's Office.

(Charleston) News and Courier. "Charleston's Resurrection," September 5, 1887.

———. "Takes Own Life in Post Office," March 27, 1924.

(Charleston) Post and Courier. "Honoring a Charleston Reporter," December 25, 2003.

City of Charleston Census, 1861. On file at the Charleston County Library, South Carolina History Room.

City of Charleston Year Books, 1909, 1919, 1920, 1921, 1922 and 1923. On file at the Charleston County Public Library, South Carolina History Room.

City of Charleston's Department of Planning, Preservation and Economic Innovation. Vertical files.

Drie, C.N. *Birds Eye View Map of the City of Charleston,* 1872. On file with the Library of Congress at: http://lcweb2.loc.gov/cgi-bin/query/D?gmd:1:./temp/~ammem_Tapu.

"East Side Patterns: A Guide for Urban Design, Charleston, South Carolina." College of Architecture, Clemson University, 1977. Unpublished document on file at the Charleston County Library, South Carolina History Room.

BIBLIOGRAPHY

Evans, Barbara Jean. *A to Zax: A Comprehensive Dictionary for Genealogists and Historians.* 3rd ed. Alexandria, VA: Hearthside Press, 1995.

Foner, Eric. *Freedman's Lawmakers: A Directory of Black Office Holders During Reconstruction.* New York: Oxford University Press, 1993.

Frasier, Walter J., Jr. *Charleston! Charleston! The History of a Southern City.* Columbia, SC: University of South Carolina Press, 1991.

Freedman's Bank Records, 1865–74. On file at the Charleston County Library, South Carolina History Room.

Garrow and Associates. "An Architectural, Archaeological, and Historical Survey of the Selected Portions of Charleston and Mount Pleasant: Grace Memorial Bridge Replacement," January 15, 1988. Unpublished document on file at the Charleston County Library, South Carolina History Room.

Geier, Brown, Renfrow Architects, Inc. "Historical Resources Inventory of the City of Charleston," 1985–86. On file at the Department of Planning, Preservation and Economic Innovation, City of Charleston.

Greene, Harlan. "Charleston Childhood: the First Years of DuBose Heyward." *South Carolina Historical Magazine* 83, no. 2 (1982).

———. Personal correspondence with the South Carolina Department of Archives and History regarding 56 Bull Street. Courtesy of Harlan Greene.

Hill, Walter B. "Family, Life, and Work Culture: Black Charleston, South Carolina, 1880–1910." Unpublished dissertation, 1989. On file at the Charleston County Library, South Carolina History Room.

Historic Charleston Foundation Archives, vertical files.

Howard, Donald S. *The WPA and Federal Relief Policy.* New York: Russell Sage Foundation, 1943.

Hudgins, Carter L., Carl R. Lounsbury, Louis P. Nelson and Jonathan H. Poston, eds. "The Vernacular Architecture of Charleston and the

Lowcountry, 1670–1990," 1994. Unpublished document on file at the Charleston County Library, South Carolina History Room.

Jarrell, Krista. "The History of 16 Council Street," 2007. Unpublished document on file at the Charleston County Library, South Carolina History Room.

Johnson, Michael P., and James L. Roark, eds. *No Chariot Let Down: Charleston's Free People of Color on the Eve of the Civil War.* Chapel Hill, NC: University of North Carolina Press, 1984.

Lamblé Block Plats of the City of Charleston, 1882. On file at the Charleston County Public Library, South Carolina History Room.

Leary, Robert M. and Associates. "East Side Design Guidelines," 1986. Unpublished document on file at the Charleston County Library, South Carolina History Room.

Mitchell & Smith. Millbrook account, n.d. (152.09.02). South Carolina Historical Society.

Poston, Jonathan H. *The Buildings of Charleston: A Guide to the City's Architecture.* Columbia, SC: University of South, 1997.

Powers, Bernard E., Jr. *Black Charlestonians: A Social History 1822–1885.* Fayetteville: University of Arkansas, 1994.

Preservation Consultants, Inc. "Charleston County Historical and Architectural Survey: Survey Report," 1992. Unpublished document on file at the Charleston County Library, South Carolina History Room.

"Record of Earthquake Damages (building damage inventory)," 1886. Found on "Materials on the Charleston earthquake of 1886" (microfilm). On file with South Carolina History Room of the Charleston County Public Library.

Reed, Phillip Edward. "Historic Houses 'freedman's cottages': Research of 111 and 113 Cooper Street, Charleston, South Carolina," 2006. Unpublished document on file at the Avery Research Center for African American History and Culture, 125 Bull Street, Charleston, South Carolina.

Riesberg, Niki. "44 Bogard Street," 2006. Unpublished document on file at the Avery Research Center for African American History and Culture.

Rosengarten, Dale, Martha Zierden, Kimberly Grimes, Ziyadah Owusu, Elizabeth Alston, and Will Williams, III. "Between the Tracks: Charleston's East Side During the Nineteenth Century," 1987. Unpublished document on file at the Charleston County Library, South Carolina History Room.

Rudacille, Lillian. "The History of 553 Rutledge Avenue," 2006. Unpublished document on file at the Avery Research Center for African American History and Culture, 125 Bull Street, Charleston, South Carolina.

Ruth Cupp Collection, photographs, undated. On file at the Charleston County Library, South Carolina History Room.

Sanborn Fire Insurance Maps of the City of Charleston, 1884, 1888, 1902 (with updates 1929, 1944, 1951) 1955, 1967. On file at the Charleston County Public Library, South Carolina History Room.

————, 1888 (updated to 1893). On file the City of Charleston's Preservation Division, 75 Calhoun Street.

Shedlock, Christina. "The History of 189 Smith Street," 2006. Unpublished document on file at the Avery Research Center for African American History and Culture.

South Carolina Death Index, 1821–1955. http://www.ancestry.com.

State Free Negro Capitation Tax Books, Charleston, South Carolina, 1811–60. On file at the Charleston County Library, South Carolina History Room.

Stockton, Robert P. "56 Bull Designated A Historic Landmark." *(Charleston) News and Courier*, August 23, 1996.

————. "Hollings Family has Maintained Ownership." *(Charleston) Evening Post*, August 6, 1990.

BIBLIOGRAPHY

Taylor, June. "The History of the Freedman's Cottage at 277 Coming Street," 2006. Unpublished document on file at the Avery Research Center for African American History and Culture.

United States Federal Census Records, 1850–1930. On file at the Charleston County Public Library, South Carolina History Room.

U.S. IRS Tax Assessment Lists, 1862-1918. http://www.ancestry.com.

Waddell, Gene. *Charleston Architecture 1670–1860.* Charleston, SC: Wyrick and Company, 2003.

INDEX

Please visit us at
www.historypress.net